Between a Rock and a Hard Place

A Somali boy growing up in Minnesota

Family, Schooling and Identity

Nuur Hassan (PhD)

Grosvenor House

This book is published by
Grosvenor House Publishing Ltd
Link House
140 The Broadway, Tolworth, Surrey, KT6 7HT.
www.grosvenorhousepublishing.co.uk

A CIP record for this book
is available from the British Library

ISBN 978-1-80381-131-4

About the Author

Nuur Hassan is a Somali-born British author and educator with extensive experience in teaching and learning, curriculum development and management in the Further and Higher Education sectors. He holds a BSc in Computer Studies, an MSc in Systems Analysis and a PhD in Education from London Southbank University, the University of London and the University of Greenwich respectively.

Dedication

To my late father, who shaped my childhood experiences so positively, and to my mother, who constantly keeps me in her prayers.

Acknowledgements

Thank you to all those who helped me collate and analyse your stories for this book – you are too numerous to list. However, I would like to mention the following individuals who helped me in the research for the book: Ubah Bihi, Abdiqani Elmi and Abdi Warsame. Thank you all.

Contents

Author's Note

My relationship with Minnesota and Somali Minnesotans dates back to 2008 when I first visited the state as a post-graduate student to work on an academic paper. My first encounter with the Somali immigrant community in Minnesota sparked a fascination with their resilience and capacity for enterprise. Despite the harsh weather, language and cultural challenges, Somalis were thriving in their adopted home. I then visited Minnesota in 2018, ten years after my first visit; this time, the progress had multiplied; the immigrant community was succeeding in business, invested in the American political system, and many were homeowners in the suburban areas of the state. However, one problem facing the community was that US-born children, mainly boys, were struggling.

The majority of Somali Minnesotan-born boys do not do well at school. A considerable number are in the criminal justice system as a result of becoming involved in gang-related criminal activity, which tends to lead to a high level of untimely death and incarceration. These gang-related crimes do not originate outside the Somali community; they involve Somali gang groups fighting each other over trivial issues. Between 2018 and 2019, it was estimated that 10 boys of Somali heritage were killed in gang-related violence. In addition to gang violence, substance abuse has risen among Somali youth in Minnesota, resulting in multiple deaths.

From the outside, it is easy to deplore the situation and become frustrated about how Minnesota-born Somali boys have fallen short of the expectations of their immigrant parents. However, the question that needs to be answered is why boys have fallen short in this way? This book is an attempt to provide such an answer.

The book draws on qualitative research conducted between August 2018 and August 2019, exploring the experiences of boys of Somali heritage between 15 and 18 years old in the State of Minnesota, USA.

Chapter 1

The history of Somali immigration to Minnesota – the genesis

Somali immigration to the USA is a relatively recent phenomenon. In the late 1960s and early 1970s, most Somalis coming to the USA were higher education students. However, this changed dramatically in the late 1980s and early 1990s, following civil wars in the north and south of Somalia, as a result of which, growing numbers of new arrivals came to the US seeking asylum. Subsequently, between the early 1990s and late 2000s, the US government admitted the largest numbers ever of Somali refugees.

The first wave of Somalis arrived in Minnesota in the mid-1990s. Owing to Minnesota's high number of unskilled job opportunities, coupled with many social services to help the new arrivals – such as Lutheran social services and state-wide Catholic Charities – many Somalis settled here, including thousands relocating from other states. As a result of this massive primary and secondary immigration of Somalis, the Twin Cities today host the most significant

1

Somali population in the US —estimated to be between 80,000 and 100,000 people.

Primary and Secondary immigration to Minnesota: adjustment and success stories

Somalis in Minnesota can be divided into two groups based on their immigration journey to the state. The first group contains those who were early arrivals or primary immigrants – mainly young single men who initiated a wave of immigrants who came as family members, joining them to settle permanently in the US. The second group is the secondary immigration – those who settled in other parts of the US but relocated to Minnesota to improve their financial circumstances. While the first group tends to have less US-based education, most of those in the second group have educational qualifications acquired in the US, some with advanced degrees. The Somali immigrants' ability to adjust to the Minnesotan way of life, and to navigate and negotiate a suitable place in their adopted state, largely depends on which group they belong to. Those who come via the secondary migration route find it relatively easy to adjust to their new homes, whereas those in the primary migration group tend to struggle to adapt.

Looking at the success stories of Somalis in Minnesota, in politics as well as in business, it is easy to see how the above two groups diverge. The majority of individuals who have reached public prominence are those who started their

American life in states other than Minnesota, including the first Somali-born congresswoman. The factors that favour these secondary migrants include, but are not limited to, English language proficiency, educational qualifications and cultural awareness.

The Immigrant Generation and the Myth of Return

Both groups discussed above are first-generation immigrants; US-born Somali Minnesotans are yet to fully establish themselves owing to the recent arrival of their parents' generation. The success of these relatively newly arrived Somali Minnesotans in becoming active participants in the US political and social landscape has taken everyone by surprise. According to Byng,[1] it is often the case that second- and third-generation American Muslims tend to be more 'invested' in the social, political and economic realities of the US – a country still considered a 'foreign land' by their immigrant first-generation parents.

The shift in the mental attitude of first-generation Somali Minnesotans regarding what it means to be a fully participating US citizen can be traced to three factors. First, there is a palpable shift in American Muslim activism, which reflects the larger question of what 'it means to be a Muslim in the Trump era, and more importantly, how to be

---

[1] Byng, 2017.

an American Muslim'.[2] Second, there is a widespread belief among Somali Minnesotans that they intend to stay in the US; the 'myth of return' to either Somalia or a Muslim-majority country no longer holds true, as illustrated by the following quotations:

'Since my arrival 20 years ago, my dream of taking my family back to Somalia has never left me. I can even say my luggage is still unpacked. However, I can now say with certainty this dream is dead.' (Somali mother)

'Even if I did not go back to Somalia, I always hoped I would go to a Muslim-majority country and leave America, but I am not sure now.' (Somali father)

'The idea of being neither here nor there – a tree without a root – meant that we, the immigrant generations, lost time to invest in the American life.' (High school teacher)

'We, the immigrant generations, have lost time by thinking that America is a temporary abode, we must not repeat this for our American-born children.' (University Professor)

---

[2] Calfano et al., 2017.

The third and final factor is what I call 'the Keith Ellison effect'. Ellison was the first Muslim to be elected to the US Congress, and Somali Minnesotans played an important role in both his first election and his re-election. This created a belief among Somalis in Minnesota that, not only did they have the power to vote someone into high office, but they could also help one of their fellow Somalis to be elected. The first election experimentation started at the local council level in the city of Minneapolis, where they elected Abdi Warsame, the first councillor of Somali heritage. This was followed by a number of state-level legislative elections in which Somali-born Minnesotans secured seats. Finally, the Keith Ellison effect culminated in the election of Ilhan Omar – a Somali-born Minnesotan – to the US Congress, replacing Ellison himself.

> 'We initially wanted to elect someone who will serve us well; then we thought to ourselves, why elect others to higher offices when we can elect one of us.' (A Somali businessman)

> 'Seeing so many Somali-born Minnesotans win seats in higher places gives the young American-born Somalis the belief that America, despite its history, is inclusive.' (Member of state-level legislative)

> 'In America, with the right attitude and preparation, the sky is the limit. Best example is Ilhan Omar.' (High school student)

Challenges facing Somali Minnesotans

Despite the success stories, several challenges face first-generation Somalis in Minnesota. Some of the key challenges are discussed below.

Generational Challenges

As the first-generation immigrants lose their control over key social capital institutions such as mosques, Somali-run schools and family businesses, the American-born generation, the natural heirs to these important community institutions, do not have sufficient ability or – according to their parents – discipline to replace their immigrant parents. In the American-born generation, boys are the most disconnected.

> *'I fear if the trend continues the way it is (i.e. the generational gap) that we will end up with a less capable second generation of Somalis and, as a result, the community would be at a loss.' (Somali father)*

> *'While girls do better, Somali boys are the lost generation, and this will have a negative impact on tomorrow's community leadership structure.' (Somali mother)*

> *'We, the immigrant generations, have done our bit to survive in American culture, but we may not have a replacement.' (Somali father)*

'Our boys are either in prison, six feet under or economically unproductive.' (Somali teacher)

'Yes, our girls are doing well, but the Somali culture is such that community leaders are largely formed by males, hence the crisis.' (Somalia community activist)

The story of the generational challenges facing Somali immigrants in Minnesota is the antithesis of an interesting story about European Jews migrating to America in the early 20th century, as described in Malcolm Gladwell's well-known book *Outliers: The Story of Success,*[3] an excerpt of which is given below:

A Russian tailor artisan comes to America, takes to the needle trade, works in a sweat shop for a small salary. Later takes garments to finish at home with the help of his wife and older children. In order to increase his salary, he works through the night. Later he makes a garment and sells it on New York streets. He accumulates some capital and goes into a business venture with his sons. They open a shop to create a men's garments. The Russian tailor and his sons become men's suit manufacturers supplying several men's stores..... the sons and the father become prosperous.... The sons' children become educated professionals.

---

[3] *Outliers: The Story of Success.*

This story is interesting because it is the dream painted by first-generation Somali immigrants. The Somali parents who came to the US with nothing and created business and other social institutions want to leave these to their US-born children so that future generations become educated professionals, better suited to American life. However, according to Somali parents, this remains for now only a dream.

Widespread unemployment and low-paid jobs

Although Minnesota's unemployment rate remains relatively stable and low compared to the rest of the US, especially in the so-called super-sectors of manufacturing, trade, leisure and hospitality,[4] the rate of unemployment among Somali youth is high. Two main factors are to blame, according to Somali community leaders in Minnesota – most well-paid jobs require college degrees and, secondly, young people 'are not willing to work hard in the sectors where there are menial jobs to do'.

Gang culture and substance use among young people

As well as facing challenges from unemployment, Somali youth are also involved in a high level of gang-related criminal activity, which frequently results in incarceration or untimely

---

[4] MDED, 2019.

death. This gang-related crime does not originate outside the community; it occurs between Somali groups fighting each other over trivial matters. Between 2018 and 2019, it was estimated that 10 boys of Somali heritage were killed in gang-related violence. Despite the efforts of community leaders and other concerned citizens to find a solution, gang violence continues to destroy young lives today.

The victims of gang-related crime are predominantly boys, but girls also form part of what one boy I spoke to called 'the leaders of peer groups', rather than the more obvious street gangs. A substantial number of Somali girls play a part in organised gangs but are not as conspicuous as their male counterparts. The following quotes illuminate the role of Somali girls in gang-related crime:

> *'Girls are part of the peer groups, they lead and help bait enemies, but they are not in the streets with us.' (Former gang member)*

> *'My friend was killed by a trap set up by a Somali girl at a house party.' (Friend of a deceased Somali boy)*

> *'Girls are not in your face when confronted with Somali gangs, but they are truly part of the structure.' (Somali teacher)*

It is difficult to know why so many young Somalis are attracted to gang membership. However, a number of reasons are cited:

Out of fear

'I was part of a gang who terrorised the streets, not because I wanted it, but out of fear of them, you're either with them or against them.' (Former gang member)

'I joined (though no longer a member) a Somali gang group under duress. A gun was put to my head, and I was forced to bear allegiance to the group.' (Somali boy)

A sense of belonging and identity

'I was very much confused, ... had identity crises and wanted to be part of a group that represented me.' (Former gang member)

School failure

'Most gang members have one thing in common, they have all had bad experiences at school.' (Somali boy)

'Gang membership is the only option open for you after you have been pushed out of school.' (Somali teacher)

Increased numbers of Minnesotan boys of Somali heritage are in state prisons serving sentences for felonies ranging from shoplifting to assault and armed robbery. The combination of these two factors alone has the potential to create a lost generation in the eyes of immigrant parents.

Substance abuse among Somali youth in the State of Minnesota is increasing, resulting in multiple deaths. An article published in 2019, by the Sahan Journal – a non-profit newsroom based in Minneapolis – entitled 'Monster in our community'[5] conveys the severity of the situation among Somali youth. The full article is given below verbatim:

> Biftu Jillo sat before a gathering of East African youth and women at the Brian Coyle Center Saturday night to talk about drug addiction — an intensifying problem in the community usually spoken of in private, if at all, and sometimes in whispers. It's a scourge she knew well. Jillo, 33, spoke of her past addiction to painkillers and warned that the Somali and Oromo communities needed to talk openly about the problems of young people addicted to drugs. "Nobody wants to be a drug addict," said Jillo, who became addicted to OxyContin at 17 after a dentist prescribed it for pain relief following surgery. "Nobody goes up and says, 'Hey, I'm going to be a drug addict when I grow up,'" she said, tearing up. "Nobody."
>
> Addiction has long been a source of shame in immigrant communities, where children's overdoses are often

---

[5] Sahan journal, 2019

cloaked as heart attacks or unexplainable deaths. Some young Twin Cities advocates are working now to push the problem into the light in the hope of saving lives. Gatherings like the one at the Coyle Center are a start. Community members say honesty can't come quickly enough.

Addiction's grip

Many first-generation Americans are at a breaking point as they straddle between their newly adopted home and the land their parents fled. In a break from tradition, they have organised and invited their friends who became addicted to drugs — considered a sin in Islam and a taboo subject to talk about in their culture — to testify to their addiction and recovery.

In September, they formalised their effort as Generation Hope, a non-profit organisation formed by youth who've lost friends to drug overdoses.

The community is finally paying attention after so many families have lost their children to fentanyl overdoses and other drugs. Abdirahman Warsame, one of the co-founders of the organisation, said they want to have open discussions about substance abuse in a safe space where youth can talk openly about their addiction.

"The only reason we are doing this is because we feel like no one would understand or care if we didn't step up to the plate," Warsame said. "Everyone that's part of our organisation, including Jillo, has had some kind of experience with substance abuse or gang violence or both. Through our stories and the community's support, everyone can feel our pain too."

Some of his co-founders got addicted to drugs before and are now sober. They held their first event on Sept. 28 after four young boys died of overdoses in a month. The group said their friends died after taking fentanyl, which Warsame called a "monster that has been raging in our community." The group plans to hold ongoing community conversations about addiction.

"We want to change how parents or the community view drug addicts and how they can support those individuals," said Khadar Abi, one of the co-founders and a former drug addict who now works at Alliance Wellness Center in Bloomington, which offers substance abuse treatment programmes.

Qalid Ibrahim, another co-founder, said he got addicted to drugs slowly, first smoking marijuana. "It got to a point where I could not eat or sleep without it," he said. "After some time, I needed to look for something new." He started taking opioids.

"After I tried it, at first it was fun," he said. "But then it got to a point where I was spending $100, 150 a day, and still I wasn't feeling anything. Day in day out, every time I would need it. And If I didn't get it,

I would get sick." Then he found fentanyl. He overdosed a few times. "At first it's about getting high," he said. "After some time, it becomes like a big monkey on your back."

'Not our kid'

Mothers and youth who spoke at Saturday night's gathering say the generational gap between parents and their US-raised children is weakening the traditional family structures. Immigrant parents, steeped in traditions, are usually not aware of the drug problem, assuming their children will never indulge in alcohol or drugs. When they find out, guilt and shame wash over them. They discourage their children from seeking help because of fear of being shunned and stigmatised in the tightly knit community. Families create cover stories when a loved one dies after an overdose.

"It's serious, and then we think it's not our kid until your kid is dead," Jillo, who's half Somali and half Oromo, told the Saturday night gathering. "We're not losers. We're human beings. We're Muslim. We're alive. We're here."

As Jillo spoke, a woman wearing a sweatshirt with the words "Health Communities" came up to her, placed her hands on her head, embraced her and kissed her on the head. Jillo wiped tears from her eyes.

"Imagine being a mom burying your kid and lying about why your kid died," said Jillo, who's a mother of four children. "You know how that would hurt?" The youth, who have a different cultural perspective than their parents, are now taking their stories public.

"Addiction is real, and it's hitting this community harder than ever because of our ignorance," Jillo said. "We just want to hide stuff. Bury your shame. Bury your shame. No. It's way past shame." "Start judging less," she told community members. That starts with the parents, said Jillo, who recounted how, after she and her mom reached an impasse, came to understand each other. "When I think of how much pain I caused my mom it just makes me cry to this day," she said. She recalled the time when she broke down to her mom and told her, "Mom, why are you discouraging me all the time? You are my mom. You're the person I'm supposed to come and talk to about my problems. I'm supposed to trust you." Her mom changed. She started listening to her daughter and pushed her to go to treatment.

"I know too many people who died that I'm close to," Jillo said. "They shouldn't be dead. They didn't even make it to their 30th birthday." (Reported in Sahan Journal on October 30, 2019.)

While this type of event plays an important role in highlighting the 'monster in our community', the stigma attached to substance addiction is so high that parents and the wider community are reluctant to seek help for the problem.

Remittance drainage and the curse of public housing

Remittances have risen spectacularly in recent decades, capturing the attention of researchers and policy makers and prompting debate on their advantages and disadvantages.[6] Miambo and Lindley (2006), writing about Somalia, noted that:

> The remittances received by a substantial minority of city-dwellers improve their economic status and access to education. In remittances often play a central role in the livelihoods of those that receive them and help finance education, in some cases allowing the family to choose higher-cost forms of education. Children in the households of people receiving remittances have relatively good school attendance rates. Moreover, migrants often encourage families to whom they send money to educate their children. Sibling solidarity plays a particularly crucial cultural role in the education and welfare of children and young people.

---

[6] Dorantes, 2014

While remittances improve the well-being of family members left behind and boost the economies of the receiving countries, researchers are now discovering their dark side, such as the creation of a culture of dependency at the micro-level and lowering labour-force participation, while promoting conspicuous consumption at the macro level.[7]

Sending money to take care of relatives is common practice for Somali families in the diaspora; they have even coined a name for these transactions: the '3 am phone call'. While there are no reliable data on the exact amount remitted to Somalia by Somalis in the diaspora, the World Bank estimated such remittances to total USD 1.4 billion in 2016. Calculating an exact amount is complicated due to the multiple channels used to send remittances; for example, some Somalis use traditional unregistered *hawala*, while others use other methods that may not leave a data trail.

While remittances act as a crucial safety net for many receivers in Somalia, they can be a drain on the sender's finances. The following quotes illuminate the financial pressure created by remittances for Somalis in Minnesota:

'My husband and I send every month at least USD500.00 to Somalia, some goes to his family and

---

[7] Dorantes, 2014; Ghosh, 2006.

some to mine. This creates a lot of financial problems for us ... as we struggle to make ends meet.' (Mother of four)

'I am a single mum with five children to raise and I am still expected to send money to my relatives back in Somalia.' (Somali mother)

'If I invested all the money that I send to Somalia in my own family here in Minneapolis, I would be financially secure for the rest of my life.' (Somali father)

'My father sends money every month to his family back home. While I understand the logic behind it, this money should have been put towards my college education.' (High school student)

'Why do you think so many Somali households rely on Section 8 and 9? The answer is remittance – it robs our chance of becoming homeowners.' (Somali father)

While remittance is generally seen as a financial drain on families in the diaspora, some see it as a moral imperative to help relatives left behind:

'We are very lucky to find ourselves in a rich country like America, we have food, we have shelter, but our relatives back home cannot say the same.' (Somali mother)

'Our remittances not only save lives, but also serve a higher purpose, which is charity; we must help our needy relatives in Somalia.' (Somali father)

'There is a valid argument to have about the long-term effectiveness of monies we send back home, but the debate should not be whether we send or not.' (Somali teacher)

Another dark side of remittance reported by Somalis is the relationship between remittances and increased immigration among Somali youth attempting to come to the West. This happens when remittances sent to some family members create envy among others who may not have family members in the diaspora, encouraging young people to emigrate to seek economic opportunities abroad. Although I have no data to evidence this assertion, it merits further investigation.

The Curse of Public Housing

'Sir, hell is paved with good intentions.'[8]

The federal public housing programme was initially part of the Housing Act of 1937, passed in the New Deal. Intended primarily as an employment and slum-clearing programme,

---

[8] Samuel Johnson, 1775.

public housing was the result of powerful grassroots pressure. Social justice advocates, such as Catherine Bauer of the Regional Planning Association of America, mobilised widespread public support for government-sponsored housing, i.e. public housing.[9] A timeline of developments is shown below. [10]

---

[9] National Low Income Housing Association.
[10] Source: NLIA

PUBLIC HOUSING TIMELINE

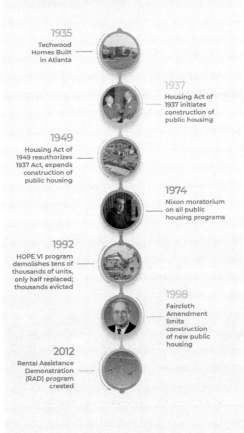

1935
Techwood Homes Built in Atlanta

1937
Housing Act of 1937 initiates construction of public housing

1949
Housing Act of 1949 reauthorizes 1937 Act, expands construction of public housing

1974
Nixon moratorium on all public housing programs

1992
HOPE VI program demolishes tens of thousands of units, only half replaced; thousands evicted

1998
Faircloth Amendment limits construction of new public housing

2012
Rental Assistance Demonstration (RAD) program created

now

Emphasis on "repositioning": converting public housing units to the private market

Despite public housing's 'new deal spirit', its critics held that the Housing Act of 1937 was a segregationist piece of legislation, whereby 'the federal government helped local governments carry out their housing segregation policies'.[11] In his book, *The Colour of law: The forgotten history of how our government segregated America*, Richard Rothstein argues that the Housing Act of 1937 legalised 'racial zoning', where blacks and whites were intentionally put in different neighbourhoods.

Figure 1: Pittsburgh, 1940. President Franklin D. Roosevelt hands keys to the 100,000th family to receive lodging in the federal government's public housing programme. Most projects were for whites only.[12]

---

[11] *The Colour of law.*
[12] Credit: Richard Rothstein.

As of 2020, the US government spends approximately $20 billion each year on the housing choice voucher programme, which provides rental assistance to low-income families.[13] Across Minnesota, there is a shortage of rental homes affordable for and available to low-income households, whose income is at or below the poverty guideline or 30% of their area median income. For many Somali Minnesotans, the cost of rent is a significant burden, swallowing over half their income. This creates a vicious circle where households 'sacrifice other necessities like healthy food and healthcare to pay the rent' yet are still likely to experience a lack of stability in their housing, including potential eviction. A Somali father whose family lives in Minneapolis public housing sums up the curse of public housing:

> *'Thanks to subsidised housing, families are trapped in undesirable neighbourhoods – local schools are bad, and crime is often rife' (Somali father)*

I wish to finish this chapter with the story of 'Salah', his family's experience of public housing and the effect this had on him as he was growing up in Cedar High Apartments, Minneapolis.

> *'I have been in and out of prison and I blame my parents who refused to move out of our crime-ridden neighbourhood.' (Salah)*

---

[13] Opportunity Insights.

Salah's story

At the tender age of 10, Salah moved with his four younger siblings – three sisters and a brother – into Cedar, a well-known social housing block in Minneapolis. Initially, all went well for Salah and his family; he enjoyed his surroundings, his father had two jobs, and his mother stayed at home full-time to spend more time with the children. However, after three years, Salah started befriending children of a similar age in the neighbourhood.

Despite his father's disapproval, Salah started coming home late, as he spent time with his new friends, who were mainly of Somali heritage. His schoolwork suffered as a result. His parents had no idea that older boys were grooming Salah for a life of petty crime and gang membership. On his 15th birthday, Salah was arrested for shoplifting. From that day, his parents lost control over him; he started smoking with his friends, fighting with rebel groups, and was arrested numerous times for misdemeanours ranging from shoplifting to mugging elderly people and driving without a licence or insurance.

Salah's parents were not passive during his troubled years. They did everything to correct their son's behaviour and bring him back on track, but to no avail. However, according to Salah, there is one thing they failed to manage – to move out of the area so that Salah could have the opportunity to start afresh. Salah's story is not unique, many young Somalis have similar experiences of growing up in public housing in areas that have high rates of both crime and poverty, and going off the rails. Salah's story has a happy ending: he is now in his late 20s, has completed college and has a good job. This ending only became possible in Salah's view when his family moved out from Cedar into a more 'decent' neighbourhood.

Moving from public housing to home-ownership or renting in areas of high opportunity, where poverty and crime are relatively low, is not easy for many Somali households. My research reveals a number of factors that trap the majority of families in public housing and areas of high poverty and crime:

- Remittance commitments
- Household size
- Unemployment or poorly paid employment
- Poor health or disability
- Lack of access to bank loans due to poor credit history
- Religious commitments

A footnote to the 'curse of public housing' is that there is a palpable feeling among Somali Minnesotans that homeownership is one way to break the cycle of poverty and crime; hence, there is an increased appetite for buying homes in affluent areas of the state.

Chapter 2

Experience 1: Parenting – overparenting, absence and confused priorities

'The way we bring up our children is mainly informed by our cultural norms, not the society we live in.' (Somali father)

Parenting, for most Somali parents, is predominantly about addressing their children's physiological needs – food, clothing and shelter. Parents also attach to parenting the responsibility for their children's cultural education and ensuring they attend school and after-school classes or Quranic lessons at the mosque. However, raising children involves more than simply meeting their physiological and educational needs. As Esther Wojcicki notes, in *How to raise successful people*:

> ... There is a better way. We have made parenting into an incredibly complicated, unintuitive endeavour, filled with fear and self-doubt. We are stressed out because we have become slaves to our children's

27

happiness. We are worried that they won't make it in this highly competitive world that we live in. We get upset when they don't get into a prestigious pre-school, or when they don't yet know their alphabet but all the other kids their age seem to know it. We are the ones who are creating this frantic, overly competitive world for our kids. In truth, parenting is really quite simple - as long as we discover the basic principles that allow children to thrive in homes, in school, and in life.

Wojcicki identifies what she calls 'five fundamental values' that can help parents to raise 'capable and successful children':

Trust*:* Wojcicki argues that parents are in a crisis of trust 'the world over': 'Parents are afraid, and that makes our children afraid - to be who they are, to take risks, to stand up against injustice.' Trust must start with the parents: 'When we are confident in the choices we make as parents, we can then trust our children to take important and necessary steps toward empowerment and independent.' The argument here is that parents need to trust themselves and their children if they are to instil confidence in their children for whatever they choose to do. Ultimately, parents must trust their own decisions. It is often said that a lack of trust in their own decision-making processes affects parents' trust in their children's ability to make the right choices.

Respect*:* The most fundamental respect we can show our children, according to Wojcicki, is towards 'their autonomy and individuality. Every child has a gift, and is a gift to the world, and it is our responsibility as parents to nurture that gift, whatever it may be'. This is precisely the opposite of telling children 'who to be, what profession to pursue, what their life should look like'; rather, it means supporting them as they identify and pursue their own goals. For Wojcicki, to respect your children is to allow them to exercise full autonomy at an early age.

Independence: Independence relies upon a strong foundation of trust and respect: 'Children who learn self-control and responsibility early in life are much better equipped to face the challenges of adulthood, and also have the skills to innovate and think creatively'. Truly independent children are 'capable of coping with adversity, setbacks, and boredom, all unavoidable aspects of life'. Children who develop independence early on, 'feel in control even when things around them are in chaos'. According to Wojcicki, independence is not a value that stands alone; it needs a foundation of trust and respect. Children must feel that they are respected and trusted by their parents. Rather than doing everything for your child, help your child to develop determination by finding solutions to their challenges – this is the central message for instilling independence in your child.

Collaboration: Collaboration, for Wojcicki, means 'working together as a family, in the classroom, or at a workplace'. For parents 'it means encouraging children to contribute to discussions, decisions, and even discipline'. In the twentieth century, when 'rule-following was one of the most important skills', parents controlled every aspect of their children's lives. In the twenty-first century, 'dictating no longer works. We shouldn't be telling our children what to do but asking them for their ideas and working together to find solutions'. For true collaboration to take place, children must feel that they are listened to, and that their ideas are valued by their parents. Avoiding dictating or giving orders when dealing with your child is key for genuine collaboration.

Kindness: It is strange but true that we tend to treat those who are closest to us without the kindness and consideration that we extend to strangers. 'Parents love their children, but they are so familiar with them, they often take basic kindness for granted. And they don't always model kindness as behaviours for the world as a whole'. Real kindness involves 'gratitude and forgiveness, service towards others, and awareness of the world outside yourself'.

TRICK – Trust, Respect, Independence, Collaboration and Kindness: these are universal values recognised by all parents, regardless of their background, religion or culture. However, every parent has a unique set of circumstances that influences their parenting behaviours. In Wojcicki's words:

> Every one of us has trauma and challenges from childhood that influence the way we relate to our children, and if we don't understand that trauma, if we don't carefully assess what went wrong, we are destined to repeat it. Failing to examine our conscious patterns and programming undermines our best efforts to raise a family based on TRICK.

This chapter will discuss two phenomena that I discovered in my research and that negatively impact Somali boys' experiences. I call these phenomena *Absent fathers with confused priorities* and *Overparenting mothers who overcompensate in their parenting roles.*

Let me first explain what these phenomena are and how they negatively impact Somali boys. Then, I will illustrate each phenomenon with examples.

Absent fathers with confused priorities

'When it rains in Mogadishu, the umbrellas go up in Minnesota.' (Nuruddin Farah)

Somalis are, regardless of their social position, by nature highly political. The clan system and social structures of Somali culture provide a fertile ground for the politics of division to flourish. My research reveals that the majority of Somali fathers in the State of Minnesota invest a significant amount of time and energy in the clan-based politics of Somalia, resulting in unsupervised homes and boys without male role models. There are two types of absent father: those physically absent and those psychologically absent.

Physical Absence: The fathers are physically not at home, or rarely at home, since they are travelling to Somalia or other places for business or politics. I will illustrate this type of absence with the story of 'Ahmed' (a pseudonym).

Ahmed is the father of three children – one daughter aged seven and two sons, aged 10 and 19 years old. He travels extensively between Minneapolis, Nairobi and Mogadishu for a mixture of business and politics. His wife is a full-time mother, and looks after the children in his absence. The 19-year-old son, although attending school and doing relatively well, has had problems with the police over alleged shoplifting and other minor crimes. The mother is unable to control her son; he never listens to her, and according to her, comes home late because he is out with his friends. Ahmed, when he is back from his trips, 'never seriously engages' with his son, he never 'sits with him' to discuss the issues that his son is facing. On numerous occasions, the two parents have conflicted over the father's lack of involvement in his children's upbringing, leading to serious relationship problems. The issue here is not that the son is rebellious; it is that because the son has never had any input from his father, he has no or little benefit from a male role model in his life.

Ahmed is not necessarily a bad or uncaring father, according to his wife. He provides for the family and takes care of them financially; the problem is that he has 'wrong and confused priorities'. His priorities lie somewhere rather than his own sons. The majority of fathers who are absent from their sons' lives fall into this category.

Psychological Absence: Here, the fathers are physically present at home but are not psychologically involved in their sons' lives. I will use the story of 'Jama' (a pseudonym) as an example:

Jama is the father of six children – four sons and two daughters. He is highly educated and holds a well-paid job. His wife is also educated to degree-level and works part-time in an educational setting. Growing up, all seemed well with the boys in their pre-teenage years. They had no problems with their schoolwork, went to after-school classes, and attended Quranic classes at the local mosque on their mother's initiative. However, trouble started when the boys were in their late teens, for one in particular. He started to drift away from school, get into trouble with the police and become involved in gang-related fights in the area. While this was happening, Jama was at home but was not aware of what was going on in his sons' lives; he was psychologically detached from them. According to his wife, Jama goes to work in the morning Monday to Friday and comes home in the late afternoon or sometimes the evening. At weekends, he occasionally drops them at the mosque, but often goes to meet his friends at one of the Somali malls.

One day, in the early hours of the morning, Jama's house was raided by anti-drug police officers, looking for Jama's eldest son for drug-related crimes.

Jama's psychological detachment is as harmful as physical detachment. He is at home, physically, giving the impression that he supports his sons, but in reality, he is absent, providing them with no role model. The number of fathers falling into this category is increasing but goes unseen by parents. Children require both physical and psychological engagement from their fathers; fathers need to be engaged in different ways – in school work, with experiences of teenage life as well as offering spiritual guidance.

Both forms of absence are prevalent among Somali fathers. However, the first attracts more attention since the absence is physically felt at home. I asked a group of mothers what they felt about these two forms of absence. Some were philosophical in their answers, while others had strong opinions about both forms (all names have been changed):

> 'My husband's absence is a physical one, he travels a lot, at times it feels that his priority lies in Somalia rather than his own family. The impact on the children is immense'. ('Kadija')

> 'My husband barely travels; he is always at home. However, he is psychologically absent, which means there is no meaningful engagement between him and his sons.' ('Halima')

> 'I would rather my children have a father at home rather than one that is absent, just being there physically makes lots of difference.' ('Rukia')

The fully involved father – the alternative

The alternative to these two types of absences is to be a fully involved father, one that is not only physically present, but also psychologically involved. To illustrate this alternative, I want to share the story of 'Ilyas' (a pseudonym).

> Ilyas is the father of five – four boys and one daughter. He is self-employed and works full-time, while his wife works part-time in a daycare centre. When he is not at work, Ilyas is at home with his

children. He has deliberately chosen to involve himself fully with their education and social lives: he constantly calls and receives messages from the schools his children attend, ensures that they are up-to-date with their schoolwork, and liaises with after-school and community centres in the city to keep him updated with current issues facing young people. Ilyas also takes his children to recreational sports – soccer, basketball and swimming. By investing so much time in his children's education and social lives, Ilyas has become an important stakeholder in his children's everyday lives. According to Ilyas, the bond between him and his children is stronger because they do so many things together. 'The trust is unbreakable, they ask me any question, I ask them any question,' he says. Problems with school, friends or personal mistakes are discussed between Ilyas and his children before they become an issue, giving Ilyas, as he puts it, the opportunity to 'nip them in the bud'.

Invitation and Resistance Factors

Why can't all fathers be like Ilyas and invest more time in their sons' education and social lives? Ilyas is sympathetic to those who struggle to engage with their sons, especially to those who are at home but psychologically distanced from their children. According to Ilyas, it is not always the fathers' 'fault' that they don't engage with their sons; their children, especially when they are in their teens, reject their fathers' attempts to be involved in their lives. 'They resist all the time; they are seeking their own independence and identity', Ilyas explains. He believes that this deters many fathers or makes them angry at their perceived rejection by their sons. 'Girls are different from boys; they are happy to allow their fathers involve in their lives regardless of age,' Ilyas adds.

Ilyas offers advice to fathers who are struggling to involve themselves meaningfully in their sons' lives: 'It is normal that your teenage sons are difficult to engage, they want their space, they want to be independent of you. This does not mean they hate you, or don't want to do anything with you – they do. Their worldview is different from yours, bear with them, don't be judgmental, allow them to make managed mistakes; gentle persistence will eventually pay off.'

The economic factor

In addition to the invitation and resistance factors, another factor impacts on the fathers' level of involvement in their sons' experience. The fathers I interviewed called it 'economic freedom'. 'Mohamed' (a pseudonym) explains what 'economic freedom' is and how it impacts fathers' involvement in their children's life experiences.

'Most of us work, sometimes two jobs. Because our jobs are not office-based, we do unsocial hours. When you do two shifts, you come home tired. It is also often the case that when working fathers come home, it is either a time when children are at sleep or when they are at school. Economic freedom is what we lack, we can't choose our shifts and the time we work; this massively impacts on the time we spend with our children.' ('Mohamed')

Fathers' impact on their children's development

Much has been written on fathers' impact on their children's development. Research conducted in 2018 by the fatherhood project[14] – a non-profit fatherhood programme 'seeking to improve the health and well-being of children and families' revealed the following:

1. Fathers' involvement, using authoritative parenting (loving and with clear boundaries and expectations), leads to better emotional, academic, social and behavioural outcomes for children.
2. Children who feel close to their fathers are twice as likely as those who do not to enter college or find stable employment after high school, 75% less likely to have a teen birth, 80% less likely to spend time in

---

[14] Fatherhood project

prison, and half as likely to experience multiple depression symptoms.

3. Fathers occupy a critical role in child development. Paternal absence hinders development from early infancy through childhood and into adulthood. The psychological harm of paternal absence experienced during childhood persists throughout life.

4. High levels of paternal involvement are correlated with higher levels of sociability, confidence and self-control in children.

5. Paternal engagement reduces the frequency of behavioural problems in boys while also decreasing delinquency and economic disadvantage in low-income families.

In his paper entitled 'Life without father',[15] published in 1996, Dr David Popenoe, a Professor of Sociology at Rutgers University, argues that:

> Fathers are far more than just second adults in the home. Involved fathers – especially biological fathers – bring positive benefits to their children that no other person is as likely to bring..... they provide protection and economic support and male role models. They have a parenting style that is significantly different from that of a mother and that difference is important in healthy child development.

---

[15] 'Life without father'

The Three Stages of Boyhood

'Boys don't grow up well if you don't help.' –
Steve Biddulph

In his book *Raising boys in the twenty-first century,*[16]
Biddulph describes three crucial stages that boys go
through when growing up, as summarised below:

1. ***Birth to six:*** The first stage of boyhood is from
   birth to six. Biddulph argues that, at this stage,
   the boy 'primarily belongs to his mother' he is 'her
   boy'. Although fathers may be fully involved in their
   boys' upbringing, the aim of this stage is to give the
   boy strong love and security and to 'switch on' to life
   'as warm and welcoming experience'.

2. ***Six to Fourteen:*** This is the stage 'when the boy,
   out of his own internal drivers, starts wanting to
   learn to be a man and looks more and more to his
   father for interest and activity'. The argument
   presented by Biddulph at this stage is that the father
   needs to build the 'competence, and skills' of his son,
   while helping him 'to become a balanced person'.
   This stage is when a boy becomes happy and secure
   about being a male.

3. ***Fourteen to adult:*** In this stage, the boy wants to
   develop his own identity and become his
   own man. According to Biddulph, he not only needs

---

[16] *Raising boys in the twenty first century*

his father's support, but also 'input from male mentors if he is to complete the journey to being fully grown-up'.

According to my research, the most crucial stage for Somali boys is the second one, although the age range is not six to fourteen but six to sixteen. It is now that Somali boys need the involvement of their fathers most. It is at this stage that boys are either made or broken. Somali fathers need, therefore, to give attention to the needs of their sons at this crucial stage. If they have psychologically and physically present fathers, boys develop confidence, model their fathers, and are more likely to become 'happy and secure about being male'.

The second most important stage for Somali boys is the final stage, 'fourteen to adult', or in the Somali case, sixteen to adult. However, this stage is almost non-existent for Somali boys in Minnesota; there are no known mentors of Somali heritage that a father can take his sons to. Yet, mentors at this stage would help Somali boys to build cultural, spiritual and educational resilience, in Biddulph's words, 'joining more and more with the adult world'.

Most Somali fathers are absent emotionally and physically from their families. This absence causes immense damage to their sons, especially during the crucial stage between six and sixteen years.

Overparenting mothers who overcompensate their parenting roles

'Everything I teach my son is then untaught by his overparenting mother – it is kushub ka-shub (I fill and she empties)' (Farhan).

My research found that Somali fathers who are absent or less involved in their sons' lives and upbringing cause significant damage to their sons' development. However, at the other end of the spectrum are mothers who over-parent their sons, and their behaviours are just as harmful as those of absent fathers. I identified two types of overparenting behaviours that Somali mothers engage in regarding their sons: helping *without being asked* and *doing too much for their sons*. I will illustrate each behaviour with an anonymised story.

Is he special needs? – helping without being asked – 'Jamila' and her son 'Samatar' (pseudonyms)

Jamila is a mother of three – two daughters aged 15 and 12 and a son aged 18 years old. According to Jamila, her daughters are very independent and rely less on her; the same cannot be said of her son. What makes her 15-year-old daughter and her not-yet-teenage girl of 12 so independent while her 18-year-old son is not? Jamila's son 'Samatar' believes the problem is not him, but his 'ever-helping mother' who smothers his independence. Here is the story of 'Jamila' and her son 'Samatar'.

Samatar, like most Somali boys, did not have a good experience at school; bright and articulate, he would get into trouble with teachers. He was labelled as a 'troublemaker' both inside and outside the class, although he denies forcefully that this was the case. According to Samatar, he talked a lot in lessons because he had 'so much to say' but the teachers wanted to hear 'none of that'; as a result, his grades and exam results suffered, although not irreparably. In his senior year, he achieved respectable grades and was expected to go to college, but did not do so.

While he was growing up, his father, whom he refers to as 'a laidback daddy', watched him from afar, responding to him only when he needed something. However, his mother was anything but 'laidback'; she would wash and cook for him and buy clothes and shoes without his knowledge. According to Samatar, his mother's overparenting behaviour continued throughout his late teens to the extent that it affected his confidence in 'dealing with the adult world'. It also affected his 'relationship' with his mother. He 'resents' the fact that his younger sisters enjoy more autonomy than he does. If he goes out with his friends, his 'helicopter' mother will not stop calling him to ask where he is and what he needs to 'eat' when he gets back home.

Does he have special needs?

Not sure what subject to study at college or what career to choose, Samatar decided to attend a career fair. His mother, Jamila, without being asked, insisted that she would come along and 'help' him to make a 'good choice'. At an interview with one of the career advisers, Samatar's mother assumed the lead in the discussion, despite her limited English language skills. Surprised by her 'domination', the careers adviser asked Jamila, 'Is he a special needs student', to which she replied, 'No'. Confused, the adviser turned to Samatar and said, 'So why are you not asking the questions? Is it not you who wants to go to college?' Annoyed, Samatar replied, 'Sir, this is what my mum does all the time. In the name of 'supporting' me, she treats me as if I am ten years old.'

What is wrong in this story?

Jamila is a caring and loving mother who wants to do the best for her son. However, she is helping her now-adult son in a way that undermines his independence and ability to make decisions. Samatar can make his own decisions; he should therefore be given space and autonomy.

Let him wash his dishes – doing too much for your son – 'Farhan' and his son 'Khalid' (pseudonyms)

Sacdiyo is a mother of two children, a daughter aged 17 and a son aged 19. Her son 'Khalid' has had troubles in and outside school. He wants to go to college, but does not have the required grades. He is a happy and polite young man but, according to his father 'Farhan', does little to help the family. He plays computer games with his friends most of the time, which 'angers' everyone at home except his mother. The same cannot be said about his younger sister; while going to school and holding down a weekend job, she is the 'second mother' of the house, according to her father.

'It is ku-shub ka-shub – I fill and she empties' – The trouble between parents

While Khalid's younger sister helps her mother with the household chores, Khalid often fails to wash up his own plates, and when challenged to do so, his mother washes the plates for him. The lack of a united voice about Khalid's 'lazy habits' has on many occasions created tension between Sacdiyo and her husband. Farhan indicates that Khalid is not a 'lazy' person; rather, his mother has made him lazy. She 'does too much for him', and 'doing too much for him teaches him to be dependent'. He plays computer games all day, has no job and is unwilling to find one. According to Farhan, it is not unusual to hear families breaking up over arguments on how to parent boys. Fathers tend to 'restrict and [be] harsher on boys' urging them to get on with life, while mothers tend to the opposite approach, often creating friction between parents.

Why are mothers overprotective of their sons?

I asked a group of Somali mothers in Minneapolis this provocative question, and the following main themes emerged from their answers:

> 'Mothers fear for the well-being of their sons... so they are naturally very protective of them.'

> 'America is very hostile for young black boys; they are vulnerable to the police, to the street and one another, hence mothers are very anxious.'

> 'Most fathers are absent, so what you see is psychologically mothers hanging on to their sons.'

> 'Most obsessions, fears and overprotective parenting behaviours by mothers towards their sons have something to do with their own childhood.'

The themes that emerged from the Somali mothers to whom I spoke depict real issues on the ground; they are not merely abstract fears, but very real, as contextualised below.

Hostility and anxiety about well-being

"America is very hostile for young black boys, they are vulnerable to the police, to the street and one another hence mothers are very anxious."

In Chapter 1, I discussed how Somali boys are involved in a high level of gang-related criminal activities, which often results in untimely deaths as well as incarcerations, and that these gang-related crimes do not originate outside the Somali community, but between Somali gangs fighting over trivial matters. Between 2018 and 2019, it is estimated that 10 Somali-American boys were killed in gang-related violence. Therefore, it is natural that parents in general, and mothers in particular, are very anxious about the safety of their sons.

In addition to gang-related deaths among Somalis, according to mothers, a Somali boy is more likely to be stopped, searched, arrested or killed by the police. There have been fatal police shootings in Minnesota where Somali boys or young Somali men were the victims.

Mothers' anxieties about the well-being of Somali boys are exacerbated by the increasing number of violent encounters between black men and the police in the streets of the US. To put into context the fear and anxiety of black parents whose boys are growing up in America, I want to share here a letter written by an African-American professor expressing a visceral fear that his son may become a victim of police brutality. Eddie S. Glaude is a distinguished professor of African-American Studies at Princeton University.

Black Father in a Letter to his son: 'I thought of you when I saw the son of Alton Sterling weeping' – 8 July 2016.

After watching the aftermath of police officers in Baton Rouge and Minnesota shooting and killing two black men, Professor Glaude decided to pen a letter to his son Langston, who was at the time reading African Studies at Brown University. Below is the letter verbatim, followed by Langston's reply to his father.

Dear Langston,

I thought of you when I saw the son of Alton Sterling weeping at a press conference. It was the latest of a string of haunting public rituals of grief. The police had killed another black person. His cries made me think of you. It seems, ever since the murder of Trayvon Martin—and you were only fifteen then— that you have had to come to terms with this pressing fact: that police can wantonly kill us, and there seems to be little or no protection. That even I can't protect you.

I remembered that day when the grand jury in Cleveland declined to indict the police officers who killed Tamir Rice. We were at an airport, traveling home. You cursed out loud and paced like a trapped animal. I didn't know how to speak to your rage. It was familiar to me, but I didn't know what to say. How could I keep it from seeping in and coloring your soul a deep shade of blue? And when I read your Facebook posts in response to the death of Sterling and Philando Castile, I felt the sting of your anger. It too was familiar. You are your grandfather's and father's child.

James Baldwin wrote—and you know how much I love Baldwin—in "The Uses of the Blues" that "in every generation, ever since Negroes have been here, every Negro mother and father has had to face that child and try to create in that child some way of surviving this particular world, some way to make the child who will be despised not despise himself." He wrote that in 1964, and here we are in 2016, and I am worried about the state of your spirit—worried that the ugliness of this world and the nastiness of some of the white people who inhabit it might dirty you on the inside. Might take away your infectious smile and replace it with a permanent scowl.

I find myself more often than not, and upon reflection this is an astonishing thing to say, no less think, wishing you were seven years old again. You were adorable at seven. The vexations of the teenage years were far off, and you still liked me. But I say this not because I find having an empty nest unbearable, although at times I do, or that I long to raise a teenager again—and eventually you would be that maddening teenager again. I just say it because I feel that you would be safer at home, with us.

Those tears, son, shook me. Diamond Reynolds's four-year-old baby consoling her mother made me tremble. I love you, and I don't know what I would do if anything ever happened to you. But I am proud to see your radical rage—your refusal to believe what this world says about you. Keep fighting. And remember, as your grandmother reminds me with all of the wisdom that Mississippi living can muster, that I won't stop worrying about you until I die.

Love,
Dad

Langston replied to his father:

Dear Dad,

When I saw those videos of Alton Sterling and Philando Castile, I thought of you and mom. I thought of Michael Brown's mother and the emotions she felt when they stole her son from her, and I wondered about the pain and anguish you both would feel if that was me in those videos. Then I, too, saw the video of Alton Sterling's son, and I thought about if it had been one of you in those videos, stolen from me by a trigger-happy policeman. The thought alone triggered emotions inside me that I didn't know existed. I wept.

I remember when I first really started getting into activism. You were always checking up on me, making sure I was safe and that I was being careful about what I said and who I said it to. I thought you were being your typical dad self, overprotective of your little boy. I also remember when I started getting death threats on Facebook and Twitter. A neo-Nazi group had put my picture up on their Twitter page. I was terrified. I ran to you.

You may not have known it then, but your presence at the time was perhaps one of the most important things that could have happened to me. On the outside, I appeared to be able to keep my composure, but on the inside I was scared. With a single tweet, my confidence and feeling of safety were shattered. To be honest, I almost didn't want to go outside. The world seemed like it was doing everything in its power to destroy me. I was overwhelmed. And despite your parental instincts, which I know were screaming to pull me off social media, you pushed me to reach higher, to stand by the right, and to rise above the ugliness I was experiencing. You taught me that fear is natural, but it's what we do in the face of fear that determines what kind of person we want to be. I will never forget those words. They motivated me. It was exactly what I needed to hear.

In these times of injustice, great anger and grief, I find myself consistently asking, "What would my father do?" Crazy, right? I'm actually listening to your advice for once. But it's your advice that keeps me going. It's what you taught me that keeps me pushing for justice. It's knowing that you love and support me that gives me some sense of safety in this cruel world. And that is everything I need.

Funny, I too find myself wishing that I were a kid again. The world seemed so much simpler back then. But then I remember Tamir Rice. I remember Trayvon Martin, Michael Brown and Aiyana Jones. I look at the faces of countless black bodies piling up in our streets. And I remember my own experiences with police officers as a kid. The struggle must continue, for our future's sake.

I love you, Dad.
Langston

Breathe: A letter to My Sons: Imani Perry[17]

'It must be terrifying to raise a Black boy in America'

In her book *Breathe,* Imani Perry – a professor of African-American Studies at Princeton University – writes emotionally to her two boys; she admits that raising black boys in America is a frightening experience for parents. Perry challenges America to see 'black children as deserving of humanity', while urging her sons and their peers to find

---

[17] *Breathe: A letter to my sons*

the 'courage to chart their paths and find steady footing and inspiration in Black tradition'.

It is easy for black parents to recoil and give up on a society that is unflinchingly racist, but that will not help their children to find 'steady footing and inspirations', claims Perry. In her book, she draws upon ideas from figures including James Baldwin, W. E. B. DuBois, Emily Dickinson, Toni Morrison, Ralph Waldo Emerson and Ida B. Wells. Perry urges black parents to inculcate in their sons *balance, love* and *hope* despite the fears posed by the American streets. Perry's book offers ways for black parents to raise boys in America without becoming disabled by fear.

Fear and moral panic in Somali mothers

The US is not a friendly place for black men; Somali mothers have every reason to be anxious about the well-being of their sons. However, this fear often prevents mothers from being rational – fear breeds more fear. When mothers have irrational fears about the safety of their sons, they tend to overparent and overprotect, which in turn leads the children they wanted to protect to be unable to function independently in society. Parents told me stories about their moral panic related to their sons, fearing that they will become Americanised and even abandon Islam if they are not closely followed. Sociologists use the term 'moral panic' to describe what happens when a society overreacts to an event or specific behaviours.

Most of the Somali mothers I spoke to experience both waves of moral panic and safety fears for their sons; these two factors alone are responsible for mothers' apparently overprotective parenting.

The missing link and late recalibration

Conceptualising Steve Biddulph's three stages of boyhood is useful in understanding the missing links in the parenting behaviours of Somali mothers and fathers. In the first stage, from birth to six years old, mothers who are primary caregivers of their sons are overwhelmed with homemaking and household chores, often running a large household. At this stage, boys need their mothers more than anyone else; they need to be taught about life and love by their mothers, but if mothers are physically and mentally exhausted, this crucial role goes unfulfilled. In the second stage, boys from the age of six need the involvement of their fathers; here, too, Somali fathers are either absent or not involved in their sons' lives.

The failure to fulfil these roles by both parents harms the early stages of the life of the Somali boy. At the teenage stage, mothers suddenly start to recalibrate their roles, focusing on their sons with fear and anxiety. This sudden shift in parenting behaviour is triggered by two factors as the following quotes from two mothers illustrate:

'Wiilasha markay yar yaryihiin ee ay guriga noo joogaan wax walwal ah nama hayo laakiin markay bilaabaan inay kaligood bixi karaan, cabsida markaas ayay nagu bilaabataa' (Somali mother). ['When our sons are young and at home, we don't worry. However, as soon as they start going out on their own, our fears kick in.']

'Teenage boys often rebel, and the first person they rebel against are their mums, naturally you want to keep them safe, so we [mothers] start overparenting and giving everything they need to stop them rebelling more.' (Somali mother)

A solution to this problem of late recalibration is for parents to fulfil the appropriate roles earlier. For example, if mothers spend quality time with their sons from birth to 6 and fathers are involved in their sons' lives from 6 years onwards, the problem would be reduced. Thus, boys would become robust and autonomous and develop relationships with their parents and beyond.

Chapter 3

Experience 2:
Beyond the family –
The school experience

'Speak to any Somali boy in Minnesota, and they will tell you of an unpleasant school experience.'
(*Somali mother*)

Schools play an important role in children's lives. Most Somali children spend 6 to 7 hours or more per day in some form of school environment. Somali boys often have unpleasant experiences with peers and teachers at school, and face a number of issues. I detail below some of the key issues mentioned by those interviewed in my research.

Schools' low expectations of Somali boys

Most of the Somali boys who took part in my research said that their school and teachers had low expectations of them and other Somali students in their school. When probed further as to why schools have such low expectations, they responded that schools believe that Somali ethnic groups do not value education and that their children require more support in English. I give below a number of direct quotes from pupils explaining what they call 'schools' low expectations of Somali students':

'In my school, most of the students are white. The teachers automatically assume that the Somalians are not as clever as the other minority children, so they always treat me like illiterate.' (Somali boy)

'I'm not sure, but especially in math, the teachers automatically presume that I can't get anything higher than a B.' (Somali boy)

Although most students expressed frustration about their schools' 'low expectations', when I asked whether teachers encouraged them to work hard, all reported that their teachers 'push them' to achieve 'good grades', as illustrated in the following quotes:

'Well, for me, math ... I say yeah, because my teacher, she's literally always pushing me, always says you can achieve good grades if you work hard ... For example, on Mondays to Thursdays every week she makes me go to her class before she starts. She always says to me, I want you to be the best, I want you to be the highest achiever in this class. You know what, I thank her for that.' (Somali boy)

'My English teacher encourages me all the time to attend support classes, and he always tells me I have a 'potential' in English, so some teachers really expect you to do well.' (Somali boy)

'Teachers do encourage often, but I'm still labelled a low achiever no matter what I do.' (Somali boy)

Deficit Model?

The students' responses reveal teachers' and schools' deficit attitudes towards Somali boys. However, other studies show that Somali girls face similar experiences. The deficit model emphasises what students lack rather than what they have in terms of cultural capital. Most Somali students are bilingual; therefore, they bring cultural capital. However, this is not valued in school. This problem is not unique to Somalis; other immigrant families face similar experiences, where schools do not value their rich cultural and linguistic backgrounds:

'Schools see our languages, culture and ways of life as a waste of space. It is either the American way or the highway.' (Oromo-heritage mother)

I asked several Somali parents about the factors they believe lie behind schools' low expectations of Somali boys. Their responses are summarised below.

'I think the problem starts as early as pre-K, the average white kid comes with highly developed

vocabulary when they come to kindergarten, whereas Somali kids come with far too inferior English language skills; the label, therefore, has started years before kids start high school.' (Somali father)

'I would say there are elements of cultural racism from teachers against our sons. Schools see all immigrant students as low achievers.' (Somali mother)

'If students don't meet the socio-economic standards of white American teachers, the expectations automatically go down.' (Somali father)

Stereotyping Somali boys as badly behaved

When I asked the Somali boys whether they had any problems at school, almost all said that they felt schools treated them unfairly as regards classroom behaviour and general school discipline. Pupils reported that they are 'stereotyped by teachers as trouble-makers' and always find themselves in their 'teachers' bad books even if they had not done anything wrong'. The following quotes from pupils about classroom behaviours and school discipline give specific examples:

'Sometimes I feel like I'm getting labelled and I'm not sure why that is the case. I normally don't have any problems, but I get labelled as a troublemaker.

If anything happens in the class - anything bad, I mean - I am the first student in the teachers' book. I think I feel I am going to hit an anger button the moment something like that happens.' (Somali boy)

'The same thing happens to me, too. My form tutor used to give me loads of detentions and letters to home. One day I was so angry that I nearly lost it. Eventually, I just walked off. I really believe that my teacher targeted me because Somali kids are stereotyped as unruly and as trouble-makers.' (Somali boy)

'I never had any problems with my school, but I know a lot of Somali friends have been excluded. Maybe some, but it can't be all. I mean, all Somalis cannot be bad, right?' (Somali boy)

I think Somalis stick up for one another and they react to situations quicker than others. Maybe the schools are racist or something; they never give us a chance. My friend, who is Somali and a very clever student, told me last year he was almost excluded because he was accused of calling a boy a 'white boy', and he said he is always called 'black', 'Muslim', and sometimes a 'pirate', and no one had done nothing about it.' (Somali boy)

'Sometimes you feel schools stereotype Somali kids and think that because our parents are from a war-torn country, so we are treated differently.' (Somali boy)

Racism

Most of the Somali boys who took part in the research had encountered racism in school settings. Somali boys bring their Somali culture and religion, which make them a target for racially motivated verbal abuse in schools, as illustrated in the quotes below.

'I am sick and tired of being told to go back where I came from?. I was born in the US, yet I am told to go back to Somalia.' (Somali student)

'My friend and I are often called terrorists, pirates and religious fanatics.' (Somali student)

'One of the problems we Somali boys face is that schools and teachers seem to perceive us as criminals and prone toward violence when we simply react to racially motivated abuses.' (Somali student)

'We feel that our schools are a culturally unsafe environment for anyone of us to do well.'

School suspensions

The suspension rate among Somali boys is very high in Minnesota's school system; students I spoke to have fears of being suspended from school by leaders who tend to view Somali boys as 'badly behaving youth'. The high proportion of suspensions among Somali boys creates relationship problems between students and their families, and between schools and parents. Home-school interaction is often minimal due to parents' mistrust of schools. Studies reveal that Somali parents prefer informal social encounters with school personnel to meeting teachers in an official format. While alternative schools are available for those suspended or excluded from mainstream schools, the educational standards are low and the amount of teaching and learning offered is very limited. Somali students do not often stay in alternative provision.

> 'Once your son is suspended from school, he is done, forget about alternative schools, they offer no adequate teaching.' (Somali mother)

> 'My son was suspended from school and placed in a nearby alternative school, the teachers didn't bother about his attendance; they have never invited me to meet them and never send me school reports - my son's education was forever damaged.' (Somali father)

> 'My son was suspended in dubious circumstances; they put him into alternative schooling, which offers neither conducive learning nor a safe environment.' (Somali father)

Charter Schools

Although the concept of charter schools dates back much further, the first law allowing their establishment was passed in Minnesota in 1991, with the first charter school in the state opening in 1992. While their original objectives are contested, the flexibility they offer to parents and students alike is widely accepted. Charter schools are centrally funded and exempt from state educational regulations. A charter school may stand alone or form part of a wider consortium operated by, for example, teacher-led, community, or faith-based groups.

Critics of charter schools argue that they do not offer value for the public money they receive, particularly in terms of quality of education and student destination. These accusations are refuted by advocates of charter schools, including some Somali teachers and parents, and there is no evidence in the literature to support such criticism. The student demographic in charter schools is strongly defined by race and ethnicity, as shown in the figure below.

Student race and ethnicity
Percent of students enrolled in charter and traditional public schools, by race and ethnicity, 2015–16

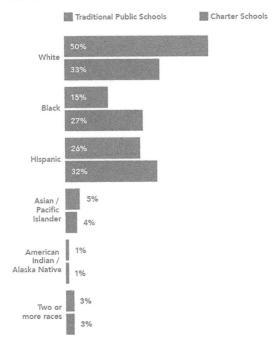

Source: U.S. Department of Education, Institute of Education Sciences and National Center for Education Statistics, *Digest of Education Statistics: 2017*, chap. 2, table 216.30, "Number and Percentage Distribution of Public Elementary and Secondary Students and Schools, by Traditional or Charter School Status and Selected Characteristics: Selected Years, 2000–01 Through 2015–16," Washington, D.C.: National Center for Education Statistics, 2017.

As shown above, charter schools tend to enrol a larger proportion of black students, bringing additional challenges, including but not limited to students who live in poverty, those with English as an additional language and students with special educational needs. The figure below shows the proportion of students from low-income households.

Students from low-income households
Percent of low-income students in 26 states, by school type, 2014–15

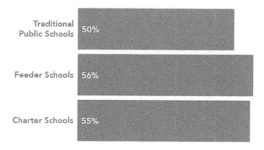

Source: Center for Research on Education Outcomes (CREDO), "Charter Management Organizations 2017," Stanford, Calif.: CREDO at Stanford University, 2017.

Providing culturally safe schooling – Somali-run charter schools

Although schools run by Somali management are more commonly elementary or middle schools, the number of high schools in this category is increasing, offering access to a substantial number of Somali students who are attracted by what one parent called 'culturally safe schooling' alongside 'high standards of education'.

According to parents, two main factors encourage Somali parents to enrol their children in Somali-run charter schools:

Language attachment

Parents new to the US, in particular, find communication with Somali-speaking school heads very helpful in their attempts to navigate the US school structure.

'Since I don't have enough knowledge about the education system of this country, I get help from the school leaders to answer all my educational questions about the school.' (Somali mother)

'I speak English but it is not adequate enough to understand the educational needs of my children, hence Somali school leaders are my social capital.' (Somali father)

'I don't have to complete a lengthy enrolment form on my own, I get this completed by the Somali-speaking professionals at school.' (Somali mother)

'Charter schools offer a great deal of support overall in the educational wellbeing of our children. I would recommend them to any parent.' (Somali father)

Language attachment is an important factor when parents are deciding between traditional public schools and Somali-led charter schools. Few Somali parents can navigate the US educational landscape, which requires a good command of the English language. The language support received by parents at Somali-run charter schools does not stop at school enrolment but continues throughout the academic year: parents receive letters and phone calls in Somali and, when meeting with teachers, Somali-speaking assistant teachers are available to help parents with their children's school reports.

'When some of my children were attending public schools, I used my elder daughter and other relatives to help me complete forms and in my communications with teachers but now that need is not there.' (Somali mother)

'I feel very comfortable when dealing with the school, knowing that there will be no language barrier between us.' (Somali father)

'When schools and teachers have a high level of cultural awareness, the quality of education increases for children; this is what is offered at charter schools.' (Somali father)

'Charter schools encourage the home-school relationship more than public schools. I have access to teachers and school management at all times.' (Somali mother)

Culturally safe schooling

For Somali parents, 'culturally safe schooling' is achieved when their children are no longer culturally in a minority in the school environment. The Somali-run charter schools offer this environment: the majority of the school population is of Somali heritage and there is a cultural homogeneity among pupils – everyone looks like everyone else, dresses in a similar way, and eats the same food. Parents see this as a safe environment for their children, rather than sending them to traditional public schools where the mainstream American culture dominates.

> 'At the Charter schools, your kids are culturally safe while getting the same educational standards at any public school ... I am very happy for my children to be here. (Somali mother)

> 'My kids have no problem at school. No one calls them [racist] names and that is very reassuring.' (Somali mother)

> 'Even white teachers are culturally empowering; they want to know more about the Somali culture so that they can embed it in their lessons.' (Somali teaching assistant)

> 'Education that doesn't take the home culture into account is not an education in my view. Charter schools empower home culture.' (Somali father)

'Ghetto education and lack of cultural awareness'

While most Somali parents I spoke to were very happy with charter schools and see factors such as 'language attachment', 'culturally safe schooling' and a 'culturally responsive curriculum' as socially and educationally advantageous, some feared that their children would not have the opportunity to experience other cultures if they went to a charter school, as illustrated in the quotations below.

'My kids are at traditional public schools, and I know there are so many challenges facing them in public schools. However, the reason I did not send my children to charter schools is for them to have a cultural awareness of wider society.' (Somali father)

'If your children attend charter schools, they will be shut off from the mainstream American schooling experience. It is like a ghetto education ... This is my view.' (Somali father)

'Yes there is less cultural hostility in charter schools, but you need your children to experience a different culture.' (Somali mother)

Challenges faced by Somali-run charter schools

Somali-run charter schools throughout the state face similar challenges. Two principal challenges stand out.

High teacher-attrition rate

Charter schools have serious teacher-retention issues: the teachers, who are predominantly young and white, tend to come and go, with the majority serving no more than two years. I asked two senior leaders in charter schools why they struggle to retain teachers and they explained that white teachers, in particular, see charter schools as a stepping stone or a 'means to an end', where the 'end' is to teach in a public school with a less challenging demographic.

'They come to us with the intention of staying two years max, then they go to public schools in affluent areas of the state.' (Charter School leader)

Charter schools are addressing this problem by providing more training to teachers to encourage them to stay longer. One leader told me that this initiative is yielding results as they are seeing more and more white middle-class teachers staying at charter schools.

'In the past, we have suffered higher teacher attrition rates, but lately we are seeing more and more teachers staying with us, but we need to do more training.' (Charter School leader)

'More culture than education'

Critics of charter schools often accuse the sector of poor performance. Some of the Somali parents I interviewed believe that charter schools 'are more about culture than education'. There is no evidence in the literature to support this claim.

'I frankly view charter schools as institutionalised dugsi ... obsessed with culture but nothing more.' (Somali father)

'Charter schools have a culturally responsive curriculum; kids are safer from racism and discrimination at least while at school. However,

when they come to attend top colleges, they will struggle with the wider culture.' (Somali father)

Despite the above challenges, Somali-run charter schools are oversubscribed, with waiting lists growing each year. The demand is exceptionally high for high-school places. A close observation of Somali-run charter schools shows many success stories and evidence that some charter schools outperform public schools, but these stories are not promoted widely by schools. One solution may be to market their success stories and student destination data more effectively, sharing it publicly with parents and prospective students. Charter schools, without question, offer culturally safer schooling and a culturally responsive curriculum for Somali children.

School-to-Prison Pipeline- avoiding the trap

In their ground-breaking work *School-to-Prison Pipeline*, Catherine Y. Kim et al. (2010)[18] explore an emerging trend that pushes a large number of at-risk, mainly black youth out of schools into the juvenile criminal justice system. They argue that certain key policies and practices implemented by schools or, as they call it, 'at the source of the pipeline', are key contributors to this trend. Some of the key policies and practices identified are 'zero-tolerance,

---

[18] School-to-Prison Pipeline

suspension & expulsion, and policing & arresting in public schools'.

According to the researchers, these policies and practices create a pipeline to prison at under-funded K12 public schools. Most Somali pupils who often live in economically disadvantaged neighbourhoods attend under-developed public schools, so we will next explore how these policies and practices affect them.

Zero-tolerance policy to 'bad behaviour'

I have encountered many harrowing stories of Somali boys being victims of a 'zero-tolerance policy', which has cost many their place at school. Somali boys often feel that 'the smallest' legitimate dissent will lead to punishment. Once sanctioned by one teacher, it is difficult to avoid sanctions from others, according to students, as these quotes explain.

> *'Just asking a legitimate question in the class will get you into the teacher's book, then from there on it is a slippery slope.' (Somali boy)*

> *'One teacher's cause for concern is another teacher's cause for concern .... I feel teachers exchange notes between them about students' behaviour.' (Somali boy)*

Undoubtedly, schools have the right to demand that their pupils follow the schools' policies and procedures;

after all, a well-behaved student body is more likely to offer a safe and educationally conducive environment to both students and staff. However, when behaviour policies are implemented as punitive rather than corrective measures, they produce different results.

Suspension and expulsion, and policing and arresting in public schools

As mentioned at the beginning of the chapter, Somali boys' suspension and expulsion rates from public schools are very high. Sometimes, parents are unaware of the school's decision and are only notified after the student has been suspended or expelled. The suspension or expulsion of a student not only affects that student, but also their family and the entire community. To highlight how devastating these policies and practices are for Somali boys and their families, I present below the story of 'Farhan' (a pseudonym), who is now in his mid-twenties and, at the time of this research, was serving a ten-year prison sentence for armed robbery.

Farhan was a bright student in his junior years at high school. He was also a promising soccer player; according to his mother, every way you looked, his future was very promising. However, after race-related altercations with white students, Farhan's family decided it was best to transfer him to another high school. Unfortunately, the same trouble followed him, but now the problem was not with students but teachers. He felt he was blamed for everything that happened in his presence; the more he was in trouble, the more bitter and angrier he became. He fought back, his reactions became very emotional and volatile, and the more he reacted, the more he was in trouble.

One day, after a verbal altercation with a science teacher, Farhan was internally suspended, which meant he would still attend school but go to special classes with students who had also been internally suspended. According to Farhan's mother, the school failed to notify her of her son's suspension; Farhan also kept his mother in the dark as, according to her, 'he finds it difficult to open up'. After the suspension period, the school decided to give Farhan a final written warning, saying he would be expelled from school if he offended again. Again, according to his mother, this final warning was not communicated to her. A few months passed without incident, and Farhan thought his troubled days were now behind him, and he could continue with his schooling and soccer training. One day, while having lunch in the cafeteria, two white pupils called him a name; he told them to 'walk away', but they repeated their insult and threatened him to 'punch him in the face'. The situation escalated and a full fight broke out in the cafeteria involving other white and Somali pupils.

The teachers were unable to defuse the fight, and the police were called. Farhan and the two white pupils who started the fight and a number of others were arrested on the spot. Although all were eventually released on the following day without charge, one of the white pupils who were part of the original altercation with Farhan pressed a charge that Farah had broken his jaw in the fight. Farhan, to this day, denies he threw the punch, saying this was someone else.

After the police released the students, Farhan's mother was notified by the police that her son had been arrested after involving himself in a fight at school. She later learned that charges were pending against Farhan, and that he was now being expelled from school by the board, with a hearing date already fixed. This news was too much for Farhan or his mother to take in. She did not know what to do but, after meeting a local attorney, decided not to appeal against the expulsion decision by the school board but to concentrate on the other charges. Farhan was later found not guilty of the accusation that he broke the jaw of the white pupil.

While this was good news, Farhan was nevertheless out of school and, according to the state's education laws, if the student is expelled from school, the district or charter school must offer the student alternative education services at another location so that students can continue to work toward graduation requirements. However, parents and students have the right to refuse the alternative education should they deem the service inadequate to meet the student's educational needs.

Farhan's mother decided to enrol him in the alternative education offered. However, after a few weeks of attending the alternative school, Farhan started to miss classes for no reason and to spend more time out with his friends. In her attempts to get Farhan back to schooling and off the street, her relationship with her son began to deteriorate, to the point where Farhan would not come home for a day or two, claiming he was staying with friends. Farhan started to experience an emotional and mental breakdown and, after a few months, decided to drop out of school without any alternative option to continue his education elsewhere. His mother, at this stage, had no idea what to do about her son's future, which now seemed light years away from the promising future he had had only a year or two earlier.

Farhan started to drift more and more to the streets; he started smoking pot and experimenting with alcohol. He was arrested on several occasions but released without charge. Then, Farhan was arrested, his home searched in the middle of the night and, finally, he was charged with armed robbery; although he was not carrying the weapon, he did take part in the robbery. He was sentenced to ten years in prison.

The tragic story of Farhan is not unique; it is one shared by many families. However, it offers a small window into the tragic outcomes for Somali boys who are expelled from school without adequate alternative education services to help them continue with their education and keep them off the street.

Parents whose children are expelled from school face multiple challenges

The first such challenge is what I call the information gap, which occurs when parents receive no communication or are not made aware of the school's disciplinary policy – which stipulates the behaviours or violations that can lead to the student's suspension or expulsion from school – or the appeal process open to students and their families. Schools are obliged by state education law to share this policy with parents and students at the beginning of the academic year. Sometimes, as one parent noted, schools do share disciplinary policies with parents, but 'parents don't bother reading them'. One reason that parents may be unable to read such documents, which are often written in professional language, is the language barrier for many, who rely on translation.

The information gap is also seen in the fact that the home-school relationship is minimal. As a Somali mother explained, 'schools prefer meeting with parents regularly', 'while parents prefer informal meetings with teachers'. If parents are unable to secure informal meetings with teachers, and this is their preferred mode of communication, the opportunity to establish a meaningful home-school relationship is lost.

Another significant challenge facing parents whose children are expelled is the lack of legal support available to them. This allows many school board decisions to go unchallenged by parents and students. Those students and parents affected by school suspension or expulsion suffer in silence with no external support.

'Dhaqan celis' as a method of helping at-risk Somali boys

Dhaqan celis means 'returning to the culture to help them rehabilitate' and is a practice widely adopted among families with at-risk young people to help them 'de-Westernise' by sending them to schools in Somalia or other Muslim-majority countries. There are two major problems with the concept and how it is operationalised: first, it rarely brings about the desired result of returning the young people to their culture, as the educational and cultural rehabilitation centres to which they are sent to are inadequate to meet their educational and cultural needs.

Second, the term *dhaqan celis* is used as a pejorative adjective to describe these young people, giving the impression that they are 'unruly', 'Westernised' and need cultural and educational correction. The society to which they are returned does not see them as victims of circumstances that they are unable to control. These at-risk young people have not received the help they required from their schools, and to some extent, their parents, to help them navigate through life.

In the course of my research, I met many pupils who had returned from *dhaqan celis* trips, and who had nothing to show for the experience; they just picked up their old habits. However, it is not entirely correct to suggest that the concept is always a failure for all concerned; there are success stories of those who have benefited from their *dhaqan celis* projects, as one Somali teacher explains:

> *'I have seen lots of kids returned to Somalia for cultural correction; while most of them don't benefit, I found out those who benefited tend to be younger 12–16 years old, and those who stay longer in Somalia with their families.'*

This quote is important for two reasons: first, the so-called cultural corrections work well for younger teens but, secondly, only if they are accompanied by their entire family. The young people sent on *dhaqan celis* tend to be older and often travel alone or stay with relatives in the destination countries, which makes the cultural adjustment very difficult for them. If parents decide to return their at-risk children for cultural correction, I strongly suggest that they plan for a longer stay, research thoroughly the educational and cultural schools in which they want their children to enrol and, above all, ensure that their child is not sent alone. I would also suggest that those who want to help their at-risk youth at home, rather than returning them to Somalia, read the school disciplinary policies and practices, communicate with school regularly, and challenge school board decisions to suspend or expel their children from school. Free legal support is available to parents and students to help them challenge cases.

The process of expulsion, the actions leading to expulsion, what parents and students need to do to avoid expulsion and the appeal process open to them are summarised below by the **Minnesota Department of Education** (accessed on 2 January 2022):

What is an Expulsion/Exclusion?

An expulsion or exclusion is the most serious consequence of inappropriate behaviour and requires school board action.

- *Expulsion is a school board action to prohibit an enrolled student from further attendance for up to 12 months from the date the student is expelled.*

- *Exclusion is an action taken by the school board to prevent enrollment or re-enrollment of a student for a period that shall not extend beyond the school year.*

When Can My Student Be Expelled/Excluded From School?

A student can be expelled or excluded for wilful violation of a reasonable school board regulation; wilful conduct that significantly disrupts the rights of other students to an education or the rights of school staff to perform their duties; or wilful conduct that endangers the student, others, or school property. Students are most commonly expelled/excluded from school for possession of a weapon or illegal drugs.

The District's Responsibility

Provide a Notice of Expulsion/Exclusion

The district must provide you and your student with a written Notice of Expulsion/Exclusion. This notice must include a complete statement of the facts; a list of witnesses and description of testimony; date, time, and place of the hearing; and a copy of the <u>Pupil Fair</u> *Dismissal Act (PFDA). This notice must also inform parents and the student of their right to obtain a legal representative of their choosing; to obtain free or low-cost legal assistance; to examine the student's educational record; and to present evidence and confront and cross-examine witnesses at the hearing.*

What is the PFDA?

The PFDA is a state law that governs student discipline. It sets out the procedures that districts must follow when expelling or excluding a student from school. It explains a student's and parent's due process rights when a student is dismissed from school.

The school district must provide the student and parent(s) with a copy of the PFDA each time a student is expelled or excluded from school.

What Happens at an Expulsion or Exclusion Hearing?

The district must inform you of your right to request a hearing. Often, you will have already received a notice of suspension, which will state the district is suspending your student pending an expulsion/ exclusion. Unless you or your student waives the right to a hearing in writing, your student cannot be expelled/excluded without having a hearing.

The hearing is closed to the public unless the student requests that it be an open proceeding. It must be held within 10 days of the Notice of the Expulsion at a time and place that is reasonable and convenient for the student and parent. The hearing must be recorded at district expense. If the proposed hearing date does not work for you, you can request it to be changed.

The hearing officer must make a recommendation to the school board within two days of the hearing. The school board decides whether your student will be expelled/excluded within five calendar days of receiving the hearing officer's decision.

You and your student have the right to hire an attorney or to have someone of your choice represent your student at the expulsion/exclusion hearing.

Consequences of Dismissal from School

If your student is expelled/excluded from school, your student is not permitted to be present at any school or district buildings, grounds, school buses, school functions, activities, or trips except for the purposes of attending an alternative education programme as part of the student's disciplinary action.

How Does My Student Continue to Receive an Education While Expelled/Excluded?

If your student is expelled/excluded, the district or charter school must offer your student alternative education services at another location so that your student can continue to work toward graduation requirements. If you do not like the services offered by the district or charter school, you can independently enrol your student in another school district or charter school (including online programmes) or a non-public school (private or home school).

What if I Disagree With the Decision to Expel or Exclude My Student?

You may request an expulsion appeal from MDE within 21 days.

21-Day Deadline. If you plan to appeal an expulsion or exclusion decision, you must meet a 21-day deadline. MDE must receive your appeal within 21 calendar days of the date of the school board action.

What Can I Do to Prevent Expulsions?

- **Read your school's discipline policy.** You or your student should receive a copy or summary of this policy at the beginning of the school year.
- **Work with your school's administrator.** When a school is in the process of determining disciplinary action for a student, they may still be willing to work with you on an alternative solution. You can ask for alternatives to expulsion. In addition, if you believe your child has a special need and/or disability, you can request a Section 504 plan and/or special education evaluation.

You can also contact your school's special education director for additional information.

- **Contact your superintendent and/or school board.** *You can raise your concerns with the superintendent and/or school board. Keep in mind that the school board makes the ultimate decision regarding expulsion and exclusion actions.*

Can My Special Education Student Still be Expelled/Excluded from School?

Yes. Similar to a non-disabled peer, a special education student can be expelled/excluded from school for behaviour that violates a district's discipline policy or state law.

Chapter 4

Experience 3:
The Somali male-female dichotomy – How boys are left behind

'While girls do better, Somali boys are the lost generation, and this will have a negative impact on tomorrow's community leadership structure.' *(Somali mother)*

Somali girls perform better than Somali boys in school and the labour market; the question is, therefore, why do girls achieve better grades in school and become more likely to find a job and go to college than boys?

My research finds three key reasons for this dichotomy: parenting behaviours, the safety net and family honour, and schools' attitudes to black boys.

Parenting behaviours – early training

'Boys lack early role models; girls have plenty in their mothers.' *(Somali teacher)*

The way that Somali girls are parented in each household and the way that Somali boys are raised play a significant role in the life chances of the two genders.

Early years – the role of mothers

Mothers play a crucial role in their children's lives, and more so than ever for their daughters. As discussed in Chapter 2, children are very close to their mothers between birth and the age of six, regardless of gender. However, after six years old, the biological makeup of boys causes them to change interests, focusing more on what the males around them have to offer. If there is no father to capture the interest of the boy, confusion sets in, because the boy wants to learn to 'be a man and looks more and more to his father for interest and activity'.[19]

This shift in boys' interests does not mean that mothers become dispensable – boys still need the support and love of their mothers. The change is just a biological phenomenon that makes a distinction between boys and girls at this early stage. Chapter 2 also discussed how many Somali fathers are either emotionally or physically absent from their children's lives due to their confused priorities. From the age of six, parenting behaviour develops that advantages girls over boys, as explained by these Somalis mothers:

---

[19] Steve Biddulph

'My daughter watches me every step of the way from a young age, she constantly learns from me, she benefits from my presence in the house.' (Somali mother)

'I have two daughters and one son aged 7 years old. My husband is not at home all the time due to work, so while my daughters have their mum to learn from, my son has no one.' (Somali mother)

'It is not that boys can't learn or be closer to their mothers; it is just their biological development that they want to do boys' stuff, hence the need for a male role model.' (Somali mother)

'Most of us don't teach our boys what we teach our girls such as cooking, cleaning, bed-making because of the genderised nature of these chores.' (Somali mother)

These quotes should not be understood as mothers abandoning their sons and concentrating exclusively on their daughters or, worse, favouring their daughters over their sons. Instead, they should be read as the product of the unintended consequences caused by the father's absence. Boys need their fathers' involvement from the age of six years old, and however hard mothers may try, they will be unable to meet the male-related developmental needs of their sons, as 'Kaaho', a qualified nurse, explains:

'Everything mothers teach their sons is gender-specific, a female perspective, this is fine for up to a period, but beyond that boys want to be a man and here is where mothers' limitations start to appear.' (Kaaho)

'From the age of six, boys start to develop new interests, they want to play soccer, they want to play basketball, and they want to be boys; this is beyond our sphere of influence.' (Somali mother)

Somali mothers see chores such as cooking, cleaning and bed-making as strictly female activities, although they are not. Boys, too, need to develop these skills to become self-sufficient and independent. In the American culture, these chores are gender-neutral, and parents encourage their children of both genders to develop them at an early age. Somali mothers should follow suit. Instead, Somali boys are shielded from household chores by mothers 'observing a culture' and are deprived of male-based interests by absent fathers, thus losing out on both sides.

The safety net of family honour

'The protection of family honour offers girls an extra safety net than boys.' (Somali father)

'Somali girls face less hostilities in the streets than Somali boys because of family honour training.' (Somali teacher)

'Mothers repeatedly lecture their daughters on how to behave publicly.' (Somali mother)

As discussed in Chapter 2, The US can be a hostile place for black men. Somali boys become involved in gender-related violence such as gang crime, with an estimated 10 Somali boys killed in gang-related violence in 2018-2019. Drug-related and criminal violence are also widespread among boys and police brutality is a daily experience for Somali boys; a Somali boy is more likely to be stopped, searched, arrested or killed by the police (see Chapter 2).

This is not to say that Somali girls are immune to the above risks – they are not. In Chapter 1, I mentioned that many girls are part of gangs who fight one another, which at times results in fatalities. However, girls are rarely the victims of this violence. Somali girls are less likely to be stopped, searched, arrested or shot dead by the police.

According to my research, this safety net for girls is underpinned by what can be called 'family honour', a code that demands that Somali girls are *'culturally correct'* and avoid anything that would shame their family's image in the community. Some girls contest the notion of 'culturally correct' behaviour, and tend not to observe it strictly, while others take it very seriously, at least in public, as this quote illustrates:

'My daughter is fully aware of the family honour on her shoulders, and she carries it well, but her friends see this as family control and are not too keen on the culture.' (Somali mother)

To 'carry the family's honour' on one's shoulders is a lesson that starts early in the lives of Somali girls; their mothers do their best to ensure that culturally acceptable behaviours are internalised and observed both in public and in private. By following these behaviours, an invisible safety net is created beneath these girls as these quotes reveal:

'My daughter, thanks to her mother, dresses modestly, comes home early and is unlikely to hang out with friends aimlessly.' (Somali father)

'A modestly dressed Somali girl minding her business is almost unlikely to attract violence from the streets ... apart from occasional Islamophobic incidents.' (Somali father)

The concept of the invisible safety net created through the notion of family honour should not be understood as constituting universal protection for all Somali girls. Nevertheless, it provides some evidence of how Somali girls benefit from their mothers' teaching and early training. By the time they are young adults, they have a maturity that saves most girls from street violence, the police and criminal activities.

The absence of a safety net for boys

Most Somali boys have no safety net for three specific reasons: first, they lack training from their mothers early in their lives and are deprived of the benefits of empowering but straightforward chores such as cooking and cleaning. Second, most boys grow up in households where fathers are either physically or emotionally absent due to confused priorities; thus, they have no male role model to learn from. Third, culturally, boys are not seen as a risk to the family image – a considerable degree of misbehaviour is culturally tolerated when committed by boys, following a 'boys will be boys' attitude. As a result, boys in their teens have no safety net to help them navigate life.

School attitudes

'Speak to any Somali boy in Minnesota, and they will tell you of an unpleasant school experience.' (Somali mother)

'While girls too suffer racism at school, boys have tough times; they are seen as out-of-control trouble-makers by teachers.' (Somali father)

'I have never received a phone call about bad behaviour from my daughters, but I have lost count of those I received for my sons.' (Somali mother)

'Even the way they dress, do their hair and walk puts them into trouble – my son was almost

suspended from school because of his hair.'
(Somali mother).

'It at times feels that schools want to fail our boys.'
(Somali father)

As discussed in Chapter 3, Somali boys face many challenges at school, frequently labelled as badly behaved and unruly. One Somali school manager explained, 'Reputation is everything, and unfortunately, the Somali boys' reputations at public schools are not good.' Schools implement draconian policies intended to curb 'bad behaviours' and 'criminal activities', but these are similar to the methods used by law-enforcement agencies in the streets, disproportionately targeting black men and boys. Threats of suspension or expulsion from school, and everyday institutional and individual racism, make the experience of Somali boys at schools hellish; as a result, grades suffer and reputation is further damaged. Schools have a role to play in positively shaping the life chances of Somali boys but, unfortunately, have the opposite effect due to their negative attitudes to black boys.

Early years – fathers do matter

'Wiil aabo la'aan ku koray qayrkii ma raaco' (Somali grandmother) ['A boy without a father falls short of his peers.']

Boys need their fathers to be present, physically and emotionally; they need to learn from them, they want to play with them, and most, from a young age, want to be like their fathers. Strong evidence shows that boys with involved fathers do better at school, attend college and become balanced adults. There is also new evidence to suggest that boys benefit psychologically from their fathers' involvement in their lives. To explain this, I want to share a short story from a doctor in Steve Biddulph's book *Raising Boys:*

> *A little boy became repeatedly ill for no apparent reason. One day, the boy was admitted to intensive care and his father, a leading medical specialist, flew back from a conference he was attending to be with his son. As soon as the father arrived, the boy got better. The father then went away to another conference, and the illness came back. At this stage, doctors were astonished and did not know what to do. A psychologist at the hospital was called in to consult on the case and, after a few examinations, suggested that the father needed to reconfigure his life-work balance, which involved being away from his son for eight months of the year. The father, feeling guilty, immediately changed his work pattern, and the boy has not been ill since.*

A note on the story

This story emphasises the importance of fathers in their sons' lives. Children who grow up in a fatherless household or one where the father is constantly absent are likely to be less balanced as adults, drop out of school, suffer prolonged unemployment or serve a prison sentence. In my research, all the Somali fathers I interviewed want to be involved fathers; they want to spend time with their sons and be part of their lives growing up. However, most are confused about what it means to be a fully involved father or how to be involved in their sons' lives. There are several ways that fathers can be involved in their sons' lives, such as spending quality time together, taking them to sports events, reading with them or helping them with schoolwork. Fathers must not see the time spent with their sons as a chore to be completed but something that is naturally fulfilling.

As discussed below, other male family members can help to provide a role model to young boys, on behalf of or alongside the father. Fathers must not fully delegate their involvement out of convenience but should only partially delegate while remaining present in the background, provided they have created the conditions that allow their older sons to be reliable role models for the younger brothers. Unfortunately, this is a rare phenomenon in Somali families. The older sons have invariably less to pass on to their younger siblings because they have not had role models in their own lives.

Older brother effect – partial delegation

'If you invest well in the firstborn, the rest will benefit, of course, other things being equal.' ('Isa', Somali father)

In my research, I found that other males regularly present at home, such as older brothers, may help boys develop their essential skills early, as girls do. However, this depends on whether the older brothers had involved fathers in their lives. If an older brother had an absent father, he has nothing to pass on to his young brother; if his father was involved, he may be able to act as a father figure for his younger brother. To illustrate the effect of older brothers, I want to share a short story of a father of three children who, when absent, uses his older son as a role model for his other son, with successful results.

Isa (a pseudonym) is the father of three children (two sons and one daughter). The older son is 20, the daughter is 12 and the younger son is ten years old. After his first son was born, Isa decided to leave his busy job, which involved being on the road driving trucks for many weeks without coming home. Instead, he took a job locally that allowed him to spend more time with his young son. According to Isa, when his daughter arrived, his older son, aged 8, was intellectually and emotionally more developed than those of the same age. Isa believes this is because his son benefited from his full involvement. Isa took his son under his wing: they went to the library and read together; they went to the grocery store together; he drove him to and from school; they played soccer and basketball together. Ten years later, his younger son was born.

As his first son became older, Isa gave him more age-appropriate responsibility while fully emotionally and physically involving himself in his son's life. Now, aged 20, the older son takes care of his young brother, as his father did; he spends time with his brother, takes him to the library to read, and plays soccer with him. Isa is a happy father who successfully developed his two sons. Finally, it is worth noting that Isa is not completely delegating to his older son his duty as a father to his younger son; according to Isa, this is 'partial delegation' to support the young boy and prepare the older son for successful fatherhood.

Note on Isa's story

Isa's story is particularly successful for two main reasons: firstly, Isa has done a remarkable job in ensuring that he invested in his first son while he was growing up, giving him a solid early start in his life. Secondly, the firstborn and his younger brother have a ten-year age gap, which is sufficient to be a role model. The age gap ensures there is no sibling rivalry between the two boys. The younger brother looks up to his older brother, rather than being a squabbling sibling. If the opposite were true, this success story would not have been possible: if the age gap were much less, the younger brother would have no model to look up to. If Isa had not invested in his firstborn son, the son would have nothing to pass on to his younger brother.

Mentorship – beyond the fathers

The years between the ages of six and sixteen are the most important years for your son: these ten years are the ones that make or break him. If you have been a meaningful part of your son's experience growing up, congratulations! You now have a balanced sixteen-year-old, confident in his male world and a beneficiary of the presence of his father from an early age. BUT, wait a minute, that is not entirely true. In fact, the most difficult time for any father starts from the age of fourteen onwards, and this is invariably the age when most Somali fathers let their sons down. From the age of fourteen, your son's hormones and physical growth make him want to break into an adult world that he is not yet ready to join. Here is where problems arise even for those fathers who were fully involved in their sons' lives. The boys start to become argumentative, develop selective hearing and are easily annoyed.

At this stage, fathers mistakenly see this as misbehaving and question their parenting techniques. They also become anxious about risks and have nightmares about American pop culture and what lurks behind it, such as alcohol, drugs and criminality. Instead of finding a creative solution to channel their sons' new energy, the fathers' response is to redouble their old control mechanisms, with more schooling and more routines doing the same thing. Here is where most relationships between teenage boys and their fathers break down or become a source of frustration.

The best remedy that fathers can adopt to help their sons is to stop emphasising the old routines. This does not mean allowing your son to dictate or choose what he wants to do, but designing new activities that channel his creative energy and passion, and doing so not alone, but alongside your son; after all, it is his interests and passions that are concerned. When your son comes on board to design the next chapter of his growth, you need a third party to join you, and this is where mentors come into play.

There are two broad reasons why fathers may need to enlist mentors; first, at the ages of 14 to 16, boys stop listening to their fathers, not because they hate them but because they want to break away from the old routine of taking orders from their parents; second, the relationship between fathers and their sons becomes tense and full of argument because two men are now involved. Bringing in a good and trustworthy mentor will stabilise the situation. To illustrate the constructive role that a good mentor can play in guiding young boys, I want to share a short story called 'Nat, Stan and the Motorbike', narrated in Steve Biddulph's book *Raising boys*.

The Story of Nat, Stan, and the Motorbike

Nat was fifteen, and his life was not going well. He had always hated school and found writing difficult, and things were just mounting up.

The school he went to was a caring school, and his parents, the counsellor and the principal knew each other and could talk comfortably. They met and decided that, if Nat could find a job, they would arrange an exception. Perhaps he was one of those boys who would be happier in the adult world than the in-between world of high school. Luckily, Nat got a job in a one-man pizza shop, Stan's Pizza, and left school. Stan, who was about thirty-five, was doing a good trade and needed help. Nat went to work there and loved it, his voice deepened and he stood taller, his bank balance grew. His parents, though, began to worry for a new reason. Nat planned to buy a new motorbike – a big bike to get to work. Their home was up a winding, slippery road in the mountains. They watched in horror as his savings got closer to the price of the motorbike. They suggested a car, to no avail. Time passed. One day Nat came home and, in the way of teenage boys, muttered something sideways as he walked past the dinner table, something about a car. They asked him to repeat it, not sure if they should. 'Oh, I am not going to get a bike. I was talking to Stan. Stan reckons I should wait and get a car'.

Thank God for Stan, thought his parents, but outwardly they just smiled and went on eating their meal.

Note on Nat's story

This story highlights the constructive role that a good mentor can play for boys of a similar age or slightly older than Nat. Although Nat's parents were at a loss when their son was failing at school, they had a network of mentors to help them engineer a new path for him, including the school principal and counsellors. Through their mentorship network, they secured Stan to mentor Nat, resulting in a success story for Nat and his family. Again, when they needed a mentor to convince Nat not to purchase a motorbike, Stan played a decisive role; without his advice, Nat would have continued with his original plan. Mentors can influence their mentees in a way that parents cannot; therefore, finding a good mentor for your son is a way to bridge the gap between the troubled teenage years and the daunting adult world awaiting your son.

Lack of mentorship for Somali boys – the missing bridge

'Wiilasha Somalida waxa la taliya markay waayaan ayay gangs ku darsamaan.' (Somali mother) ['A lack of mentorship means Somali boys joining gangs.']

I have surveyed the mentorship landscape in Minnesota and failed to find one that adequately addresses the needs of Somali boys. This lack of mentorship for Somali boys in the state means that at-risk youth are unable to find guidance beyond families. As discussed above, from

14–16 years, boys want to develop their own identity, separate from their families. When this happens, the parents' response is frustration, and the introduction of more educational routines and cultural correction (*dhaqan celis*). The more these are applied, the more boys resist and the further they drift from their families. When boys are at this age and attempting to create their own identity, parents should carefully and watchfully ease back and bring in a culturally and spiritually suitable mentor. If there are no good mentors available to bridge the gap, it will be bridged by their peers and the street, with catastrophic results.

Choosing a mentor for your son – what to look for

Parents must lead the process of finding a mentor, they must ensure that the adult they choose to mentor their son is a balanced person, culturally and religiously. Somali-run social groups, Masjid groups, family-friendly sports clubs and community centres are good places to start when seeking a suitable mentor.

Mentors are not intended to act as second parents; they are adults outside the family with fresh and interesting ideas to shape your son's worldview. Some of the dilemmas that young people experience are career choices, relationships and identities; these are big and complex questions that require carefully crafted mentorship. As any parents know, regardless of the relationship they have with their sons, there are some things that sons will never discuss with their parents.

One of the misconceptions about mentors among Somalis is that mentors are like teachers who bridge the educational gaps for at-risk youth. This is not the case: a mentor is someone with certain experience and knowledge in a given domain or domains who can motivate, train and advise less-experienced mentees. A business owner can act as mentor for a young person in their career in business, money management and investment; a retired teacher may mentor young boys aspiring to go to college or wanting a career in the education sector.

There are a number of benefits that a good mentor can offer to your son, including constructive criticism, personal growth, a role model, encouragement and advice, trade skills, career guidance and network connections. When choosing a mentor for your son, ensure that the mentor is not another teacher acting as a supplementary tutor; your son needs someone with wider interests and expertise beyond formal education.

A final thought

Mothers need to teach their sons to do household chores at an early age. Helping with the cleaning, cooking and bed-making alongside their mothers or sisters will give boys confidence and life skills. Fathers need to be there for their sons from the ages of six to sixteen, helping them to grow and enjoy being male. When boys seek to break into the adult world from fourteen onwards, parents must seek good and balanced mentors to guide, encourage and teach their sons, while remaining fully involved.

Chapter 5

Experience 4:
Multi-hyphenated identity –
which side of the hyphen?

*'I don't know my identity, I am conflicted, I am
in-between I guess.' (Somali boy)*

*'I am one of many, I am Somali, I am an American, I
am Muslim and I am black.' (Somali boy)*

As discussed earlier, Somali boys face myriad challenges
growing up, from absent fathers and the lack of male role
models to hostile school systems and racism. However, the
identity crisis is the most significant and enduring challenge
to face Somali boys growing up in Minnesota. This identity
crisis is most acute during adolescence, when boys are
forming and discovering themselves. As the above quotes
show, Somali boys are torn between their Somali cultural
identity, on which their parents insist and to which they
desperately cling, and the American identity imposed by
their peers and the dominant culture.

To illustrate the identity crisis that Somali boys experience,
and their attempts to negotiate these different cultures, I

want to tell a short story of how one boy reconciles the cultural demands imposed by his parents with the dominant culture.

Jacket-switching – fitting in both worlds

'I am Somali by heart, American by appearance, but invested in both.' ('Abdi', a Somali boy)

Abdi (a pseudonym) is a balanced eighteen-year-old boy who is doing very well in his final year of high school. He intends to go to law school and become a district attorney. Abdi's home life is a 'traditional' one, in which parents generally expect their children to do well in school, stay away from the troubles brought by American popular culture, go to college and have a stable career and a family. However, Abdi is anything but 'traditional' in the way his parents want – he loves the American popular culture of sports, music and movies, independence, going out and eating out. While Abdi loves America, he is not ready to abandon his Somali identity, and here he has to find a way to reconcile two polar cultures into one identity? Abdi's strategy is, he says, a simple but effective 'two jacket strategy' that enables him to fit into both cultures. Abdi has two imaginary jackets, each only visible to its intended audience. One jacket is for the dominant culture and the other fits his home culture and Somalinimo

(Somaliness). According to Abdi, when he is with his family and the wider Somali community, he puts on his home jacket, which means doing all that is expected of him within Somali culture. However, when he is with his American – or Americanised Somali – friends he duly dons his American jacket, embracing American pop culture. Thus, he is 'accepted in both worlds'.

According to Abdi, switching between the two jackets is no mean feat; the exercise carries the risk of being 'busted by parents and the community' and also requires him to be constantly in 'different time zones'. For Abdi, 'jacket-switching' requires a genuine and equal investment in both cultures, 'one must be equally interested in the richness of both cultures' and 'avoid the indulgence of one culture more than the other'. While the balancing act between the two cultures is difficult, Abdi believes it is possible to be 'fully American while remaining fully Somali'. According to Abdi, young Somalis fail to negotiate the two cultures, hence the crisis, because they gravitate towards the American culture which results in a backlash from families, increasing the alienation crisis among young people.

Abdi admits the 'jacket-switching' strategy is not for everyone, because the amount of acting involved is beyond the commitment of most boys. 'Somali boys want to enjoy the freedom the American culture offers,' he explains, but this freedom has a high price tag, which is 'family conflict'. While Abdi is unwilling to talk about others in his peer group, he said that Somali girls at high school are 'expert in jacket-switching more than boys' and 'successfully remain hidden' from their families.

Note on Abdi's story.

'I am Somali by heart, American by appearance but invested in both.' (Abdi, Somali boy)

Abdi's story depicts a boy going through a series of identity conflicts, one who wants to remain in his ethnic culture and also fit within the dominant culture. However, while switching jackets may appear a valuable strategy to Abdi and others, the practice has a long-term adverse effect on the identity of today's youth and tomorrow's adults. The emotional ambiguity of living in-between creates what the Cuban scholar Gustavo Perez calls the 'one-and-a-half generation' because they are 'marginal to both cultures'. For the Somali diaspora, this generation is pejoratively labelled as the 'Say walaahi generation', roughly translated as 'those who are not culturally fully Somali.'

However, looking at this problem from a different angle, some argue that to be part of both worlds is an advantage, as the following quotes from Somali parents explain.

'We don't need a segregated generation; we want our children to fully invest in the American life while not abandoning their Somali culture.' (Somali father)

'There has to be give and take in both cultures; you can't keep your child in the Somali culture alone when in America – you take something, and you give something in return.' (Somali mother)

'Identity crisis is real among Somali youth, especially for those at-risk; the best way to address this is not to isolate the children more, it is to carefully embrace the good, and leave the bad of American culture.' (Somali businessman)

These views are not necessarily widely held among Somali parents and professionals. Every Somali parent's dream is to preserve their Somali identity and culture in their children; they fiercely resist the assimilation and 'Americanisation' of their children. The question, therefore, is how to 'preserve the Somali culture in your children' without imposing alienating restrictions on them. As one parent noted, 'It is rather futile to expect that the dominant culture will not influence your American-born child'. Recommendations for parents on how to best address the identity crisis that children experience are provided at the end of the chapter. First, however, let us look at the genesis of why Somali boys have an identity crisis.

Identity and home – the diasporic effects

Since the Somali civil war started in the early 1990s, Somalis have dispersed to all corners of the globe. There are now huge diaspora communities in the major continents of the world – Europe, North America, Australia and Asia. While the economic and political conditions of Somalis in diaspora differ vastly, they all share the common conditions of exile and displacement, a feeling that they are living in a foreign land and a hope that one day they will return to Somalia permanently. This sense of displacement and living in-between makes hard it for the community to address the question of identity, especially when this is raised by immigrant children who do not share the same feelings of displacement and exile as their parents.

In her 1993 essay 'Defining Genealogies: Feminist Reflections on Being South Asian in North America',[20] Chandra Mohanty asks:

> What is home? The place I was born? Where I grew up? Where I lived and worked as an adult? Where I locate my community and my people?

These are profound questions that, if addressed thoughtfully, can help parents better understand the identity crisis ripping apart Somali youth in the diaspora. For a Minnesotan-born Somali boy, the question of home is

---

[20] Defining Genealogies.

simple – it is where he was born and grew up, and that is the State of Minnesota. Unfortunately, for the parents, this is not the case: their home is firmly located in Somalia, their country is Somalia, and their community and people are in Somalia. Of course, this is not to say that all Somali parents view the US as a temporary dwelling, for they do not, but it is, without doubt, the majority view.

The myth of return is still potent among first-generation immigrants. It is not uncommon for parents to take their children out of school for an extended period to visit Somalia or other parts of Africa to maintain the connection. It is also not uncommon to hear parents planning to buy retirement homes in Somalia and leave the US for good. While the immigrant generation may want to return to their homeland, two factors stand in their way: the economic factor, in that most families are financially unable to relocate to a country largely dependent on humanitarian assistance and remittance handouts and, secondly, the political factor, for Somalia is politically relatively unstable and thus not a good destination for many diaspora families.

The following quotes exemplify the dilemma parents face when deciding where home is

'Although I have been in Minnesota for twenty years, my luggage is still packed as I want to go back to

Somalia, but the conditions are not right.' (Somali mother)

'I want to go back but I have no stable country to go back to; I feel we are stuck here.' (Somali mother)

'If I move my family back to Somalia, who is going to pay my bills? There are no jobs for me and no income.' (Somali father)

The two shades of acculturation resistance by immigrant generations

Somali parents who fear their children will be Americanised but cannot, for economic and political reasons, permanently relocate to Somalia tend to adopt two pushback strategies to confront the tide of Americanisation. Below, each strategy is explained with examples.

Dhaqan Celis – Parents' tool to push back against acculturation

As discussed in Chapter 3, *dhaqan celis* means 'returning to the culture to help them rehabilitate'. The practice is widely adopted by families with at-risk youth to help them 'de-Westernise' their children by sending them to schools in Somalia or Muslim-majority countries. However, it raises two significant problems: first, the practice rarely brings the desired result of returning at-risk young people to their culture. The educational and cultural rehabilitation centres to which the children are sent are inadequate to meet their academic and cultural needs. They are often sent to relatives who speak no English and have less understanding about the American culture in which these young people grew up. Second, the term *dhaqan celis* is in itself derogatory, implying the young people are unruly, Americanised and need cultural and educational correction. The society to which they are returned does not see that they have been sent back because of their parents' perception of Western culture, which is beyond their control.

Dhaqan celis may work in specific circumstances, for example, if the child is young, and the receiving relatives and institutions are able to provide adequate cultural education. However, for the majority of boys sent back to Somalia for cultural correction, the relocation only makes the matter worse. Below is the story of *Nadiir* (a pseudonym), who was sent to Kenya for cultural correction.

Nadiir's story

Nadiir was fourteen years old when his parents started to realise that he was a handful, arguing with his parents, fighting with his siblings and not doing his school work on time. Nadiir questioned everything. Despite his parents' 'moral panic', his teachers were convinced that he was a good pupil

114

with strong academic potential. According to his father, he started skipping prayers, especially 'fajar' prayers. He spoke less Somali at home and refused to have his hair cut in a style his parents wanted. Because Nadiir was popular at school he had many friends from both genders and from all races. At home, he spent time in his room playing on his Xbox console with his friends online and offline. Nadiir's parents grew more and more anxious as time passed. Just before Nadiir's sixteenth birthday, his parents decided to take him to Kenya for an extended vacation and cultural correction. To avoid Nadiir suspecting anything was amiss, the whole family flew to Kenya on a family holiday. This was the first time that Nadiir had seen Africa so, according to his father, he was 'very excited' to visit Kenya and his grandparents who lived there. After four weeks in Kenya, the rest of the family, except Nadiir and his father, returned to Minnesota.

When Nadiir heard that he was to stay in Kenya for the foreseeable future, he was very angry and refused to speak to his father or mother for days. Eventually, Nadiir accepted his new home and was enrolled in a local school. The first few months seemed to go well and Nadiir seemed to have settled well in his new environment. His father returned to Minnesota, since the family depended on his earnings from his transport company. A few weeks after the departure of his father, Nadiir started to skip school, hang out with other boys who had been sent back from Europe for cultural correction, and started getting into trouble with local gangs and the police. As time passed, Nadiir become so hard for his grandparents to handle that his father had to return to Kenya to sort his son out.

Eventually, after long discussions between Nadiir's father and grandparents, it was decided that Kenya was more dangerous to Nadiir than Minnesota. After eighteen months, Nadiir returned to Minnesota, more traumatised, angry with his parents and with two years' educational deficit.

Note on Nadiir's story

Nadiir's story is not unique; many boys like Nadiir – and younger – had their education massively disrupted through *dhaqan celis* that are rarely successful because parents had no solution to deal with their children's identity crisis. The best course of action for boys like Nadiir is to address the causes of the crisis head-on, rather than run away or morally panic. Boys in their teens and pre-teens go through many developmental crises. Their brains are transitioning from childhood to adulthood, and parents need to exercise patience and understand the inner turmoil these age groups are going through.

As discussed in Chapter 4, fathers must invest in their sons' lives from the age of six. If boys had male role models in their fathers or older brothers, followed by proper mentorship, the identity crisis would be less devastating. However, if boys grow up in a fatherless household or one where the father is less involved, the identity crisis and associated troubles are compounded. Nadiir needed understanding, patience, an outlet for his energy, mentorship and, above all, emotional investment from his father, not *dhaqan celis*.

The family moves but the father remains behind.

In this strategy, the family moves to Somalia or another Muslim-majority country while the father remains in Minnesota to support the family financially. This is a very popular anti-acculturation strategy for two reasons: first, the move is economically feasible as the fathers remain behind to support the family. Second, the child does not feel singled out since the entire family is with him and supports him while away from America. However, like the first strategy, this also brings with it a number of challenges, as the following quotes from parents show:

'My family spent 3 years in Somalia, and while the children have culturally benefited from the move, it was a struggle for me financially.' (Somali father)

'Most of the families spend a few years outside America and come back, which means the children can easily readjust to their old American lives.' (Somali teacher)

'I see these moves as temporary moves, with no benefits but disruption.' (Somali mother)

'Not every family can afford this extended holiday. I had two jobs for five years while my kids and wife were away in Egypt.' (Somali father)

As the above quotes highlight, the financial burden of supporting families abroad while maintaining a home in Minnesota for their future return is beyond many low-income families. Unlike in the US, housing, schooling and healthcare are not free or subsidised in Somalia for low-income families. Because families are unable to maintain the move permanently, they tend to return to Minnesota after two to three years; they are not away long enough to reform an identity, and most of the children are quick to readjust when they return to Minnesota. Most of the costs incurred by families come in the form of housing and education, since families tend to rent high-value properties and want to send their returned children to private schools with high tuition fees.

A multi-hyphenated identity –
the unique position of Somali boys

A multi-hyphenated identity is similar to a hyphenated identity but with more layers. A hyphenated identity is what sociologists describe as 'duality' or a dual identity, which indicates that a person straddles two cultures. A multi-hyphenated identity describes a person with more than two identities. For example, where hyphenated identity would describe a Somali boy as Somali-American, the multi-hyphenated identity would make him Somali-Muslim-African-American. These multi-hyphenated competing identities are too heavy for Somali boys to carry. The problem is not the multi-hyphenated identity itself, but the need to reconcile them or choose one over the other that creates the crisis, as the following quotes explain.

> *'Our parents don't understand that we are carrying identity weights on our shoulders; I have to be Somali, then Muslim, Black and then American. This is not an easy game.' (Somali boy)*

> *'I don't want to disappoint my parents, but I also want to remain relevant in the dominant culture; how do you reconcile that?' (Somali boy)*

> *'I truly want to be Somali, Muslim, Black and American, but I am only one person.' (Somali boy)*

In attempting to navigate these hyphenated identities, Somali boys often find it difficult to reconcile the Somali side of the hyphen and the American side, because the two cultures are polar opposites and have no common ground. According to the boys, if you take something from the American culture, you have to give something of your Somali culture away, and this is 'where conflict with parents starts', as the following quote illustrates.

> 'Our parents are happy for us to do well at school, speak better English, go to college and get a good and well-paid job. However, the first casualty of doing well at school, speaking better English and aspiring to get a corporate job is your mother tongue; as soon as you lose your Somali tongue or become bad at it, parents are triggered and the panic of acculturation starts.' (Group of Somali boys)

In addition to the loss of the mother tongue, changes to dress, hairstyle and entertainment such as music also cause parents to make snap judgements about their children's acculturation. Dress is an issue for both genders: although parents find it most traumatic when girls dress in a Western-style, boys can also attract disapproval. The loss of the Somali language and change of dress, particularly by girls, carry stigma in the Somali community, and parents do whatever they can to avoid this social stigma. As one parent said, 'No one wants their children treated as cultureless by the community'. The social stigma associated with the loss of culture has implications for the children's marriage and or relationship prospects with other Somalis, and this is important for any parent as Somalis place great emphasis on marriage and relationships.

I asked a group of Somali parents why the loss of mother tongue and change of dress and hairstyle are redlines for the 'Americanisation' of their children, and give their responses below, verbatim.

> *'Once your child loses his/her mother tongue you have lost that child, language is essential for who you are.' (Somali mother)*

> *'Language, and dresses, are symbolic for who we are and once you lose them you lose your identity.' (Somali father)*

> *'Our survival as a Somali community depends on our children's choice of identity; if they maintain their language, religion and culture, we survive, but if they don't, God help us.' (Somali mother)*

Mental health – the product of the identity crisis

Studies show that mental illness is prevalent among Somali boys in Minnesota. While the causes of the illness vary from one child to another, parents and community leaders believe that identity crisis is the biggest contributor to mental health problems. 'If a boy is confused and feels marginal to the dominant culture while not confident enough in his home culture, he may get angry or depressed, leading to other undesired habits such as doing drugs and drinking,' said a Somali teacher. Unfortunately, studies show that mental illness is seen as a stigma among Somali Minnesotans and is barely taken seriously until it is too late.

To illustrate this, I want to share a short story about 'Hussein' (a pseudonym) who ended up in hospital and was still recovering from a serious mental illness at the time of writing, after going through what his parents described as a series of identity conflicts.

Hussein's story

Hussein was 17 years old at the time of the research. Just before his sixteenth birthday, he started having problems at school, which led him to skip classes, and was almost excluded. His relationship with his parents and siblings had also begun to deteriorate: he was arguing and fighting with them all the time and refused to come home after school, often returning very late at night. According to his parents, the problem was not only school: he also started listening to 'gangster music' at home and refused to pray, at times questioning his Islamic faith, his Somali culture and everything his parents held dear. They also suspected that he had started smoking.

Just before his seventeenth birthday, Hussein began to exhibit strange behaviour, which made his parents more anxious. One day, he refused to go out and locked himself in his room, saying that someone was after him and would harm him.

His parents tried to take him to the doctors, but Hussein refused their help. They suggested moving him to Somalia to change environment, but again he refused their offer. As time passed, Hussein's health worsened, and he stopped taking showers, brushing his teeth and eating. After a difficult few months, Hussein started to experience hallucinations, panic attacks, and became suspicious of his own family. Finally, with the help of a family friend, Hussein was taken to a psychiatric hospital, where he was admitted and diagnosed as suffering from severe mental health issues. At the time of this research, Hussein was recovering from his illness and was taking antipsychotic medication at home.

While Hussein is lucky to have received professional help, many Somali boys suffer immensely without help. Parents refuse to accept the condition, for fear of social stigma or misdiagnosis. Moreover, boys may refuse help since one of the symptoms of mental illness is a refusal to believe there is a problem. These combined factors add to the mental health crisis among Somali boys in Minnesota. If mental health problems are not addressed early, there are serious risks to the lives of these young boys and the wider community.

Identity crisis – the solution

The identity crises facing Somali boys are real. All the boys I surveyed were genuinely interested in maintaining their Somali culture, but were also interested in investing in American culture to remain 'relevant within their peer group'. Satisfying two opposing cultures at the same time is no mean feat, and boys do struggle. Somali boys are concerned about their parents' poor insight into their struggles, as parents often dismiss an identity crisis as a 'choice' that needs 'discipline'. If the child is well disciplined, he 'should delineate boundaries between the two cultures', and make the 'correct choice'. The correct choice often means the 'rejection of the American side of the hyphen without question'.

This is not the way to address a problem as complex as the identity crisis. To alleviate the burden and mitigate the impact of identity crisis among Somali Minnesotan boys, parents should invest in the following.

Contextual understanding

Parents must understand that their sons live in a dominant culture; the American popular (Pop) culture is pervasive throughout the world and is a very attractive and powerful brand. Somali boys find the entertainment aspect of the culture – the music and movies – appealing, likewise the emphasis on the individual rather than the collective. The Somali culture focuses on the collective of the family and community and sees culture as driven by a collection of people, not individuals; in other words, the emphasis is on the family, not the individual, in Somali culture.

In contrast, American culture focuses on the individual rather than the collective, and parents should therefore be philosophical about the individual rather than the collective. If a person is successful at the individual level, the collective benefits first and foremost. It is also worth parents noting that their adolescent sons are quicker to pick up the culture than their immigrant parents; for example, they learn the language quicker than their parents, which inevitably disturbs family dynamics, and this should be viewed within the wider cultural context of living under a dominant culture.

Relationship with your son

In addition to a contextual understanding of the culture in which your son is growing up, you need to forge a relationship with him that allows a frank discussion of identity and American culture. Your son must trust you with his vulnerabilities; he must know that if he is honest about his feelings and relationships and mistakes within the American cultural context, he will not be met with harsh treatment but, rather, understanding and sympathy. This is a very difficult relationship to develop between Somali boys and their fathers for two main reasons. First, the majority of fathers concentrate on the physiological side of parenting, in other words providing shelter, food and clothing, rather than the emotional side. Emotional parenting is simply investing in your son's emotions, his interests, expectations and fears. Secondly, boys often view their fathers as r ule-enforcers rather than people with whom they can negotiate boundaries. This rule-based relationship between father and son is sterile, lacking in emotion and not conducive to trust. This is not to say that Somali boys do not trust their fathers, but that this type of trust is not such that a Somali boy would be comfortable discussing his vulnerability or sensitive feelings with his father, as shown in the following quotes:

'While I would like to speak freely to my father about everything, I can't because there are boundaries between me and my father.' (Somali boy)

'I don't have the confidence to freely express my feelings to my father; our fathers are less emotional and we internalise that feeling.' (Group of Somali boys)

'It is difficult to express my emotions or sensitive feelings to my father, not because I don't trust him, it

is because of the fear of disappointing him and also embarrassing myself.' (Somali boy)

American pop culture is more appealing than parents' routines

As discussed earlier, American culture is a global brand, more widely followed than any other culture in the world. Entertainment, sports, music and fashion are the pillars that make American culture so appealing to young boys of any ethnicity. Somali boys want to go to the cinema, attend sports events and listen to their favourite rhythm and blues music. In contrast, the dream of any Somali parent is to avoid interaction between their children and these cultural pillars. In reality, this is a difficult battle to win. The parents' preferred method of countering interaction with American culture is to add more of the same – to go to school and come straight home, to dress according to Somali cultural norms, and go to Dugsi and mosques for prayers. While these have undoubted merits, they are less appealing to most young boys. Without succumbing to the proverbial 'if you can't beat them, join them', parents should be more flexible and accommodating in their routines, as shown in the quotes below.

'Our parents want us to be doctors, engineers and memorise the Quran at the same time without making experiences fun.' (Somali boy)

'My dad considers anything outside education a failure. I am interested in soccer, am I a failure?' (Somali boy)

'Flexibility and understanding is what we need from our parents. What would they have done if they were in my shoes?' (Somali boy)

Final note

When navigating multiple identities, questions such as loyalty and acceptance are the greatest challenges facing Somali boys. They face racial discrimination from the dominant culture as they are not seen as 'fully American'. They also face pressure from their parents and families. Family pressure combined with racial discrimination and a lack of acceptance as 'true Americans' often breed more frustration and alienation among Somali boys. As one boy succinctly put it, 'they are neither here nor there'. All parents need to understand this and mitigate its effect on their sons.

Chapter 6

Conclusion: Managing the experiences of Somali boys in Minnesota

Chapter 6 serves, first, to recapitulate the previous five chapters and, second, to provide recommendations for managing the experiences of Somali boys in Minnesota.

What do we need to know about the history of Somali immigration to Minnesota?

Somali immigration to the US is a relatively recent phenomenon. Most Somalis arriving in the late 1960s and early 1970s were higher education students. Numbers increased in the 1990s due to the civil war in Somalia, with new arrivals seeking asylum, followed by further waves through the first decade of the 21st century.

Somalis came directly to Minnesota until the late 1990s when their numbers were swelled by internal immigrants from other states, attracted by Minnesota's unskilled job opportunities and strong social service support for new arrivals. As a result, the Twin Cities today are home to up to 100,000 Somalis, the largest Somali population in the US.

Adjustment and success stories

Somalis in Minnesota can be divided into primary immigrants – including the first arrivals who were mainly young, single men who later brought their families to settle permanently in the US, and secondary immigrants, who initially settled in other parts of the US but relocated to Minnesota for financial reasons. While the first group tends to be less educated, the second group mostly have educational qualifications acquired in the US, including some with advanced degrees. The Somali immigrants' adjustment to the Minnesotan way of life largely depends on which group they belong to: those relocating from other states find it easier than those in the primary group largely due to their superior English language proficiency, educational qualifications and cultural awareness. Looking at the success stories of Somalis in Minnesota, it is easy to see how the above two groups diverge. Most Somali Minnesotans who have assumed prominence in the state lived previously in other states, including the first Somali-born congresswoman.

The myth of return hampers first-generation immigrants in Minnesota

The two groups discussed above are both first-generation immigrants; US-born Somali Minnesotans are yet to fully establish themselves owing to the recent arrival of their parents' generation. The success of these relatively newly arrived Somali Minnesotans in becoming active participants in the US political and social landscape has taken everyone by surprise. According to many studies, the US-born generation tends to do well as they invest in US life socially, politically and economically. In contrast, the immigrant generation considers itself exiled and only temporarily in the US, but this is not the case for Somalis:

> 'Since my arrival 20 years ago, my dream of taking my family back to Somalia has never left me. I can even say my luggage is still packed. However, I can now say with certainty this dream is dead.' (Somali Mother)

> 'Even if I did not go back to Somalia, I always hoped I would go to a Muslim-majority country and leave America, but I am not sure now.' (Somali Father)

While the majority of the immigrant generation harbour a feeling of 'exile', some see this nostalgia as an impediment to being fully invested in American life:

'The idea of being neither here nor there – a tree without a root, meant we, the immigrant generations, lost time to invest in the American life.' (High school teacher)

'We, the immigrant generations, have lost time by thinking that America is a temporary abode; we must not repeat this for our American-born children.' (University Professor)

Investing in American politics

After helping elect a number of high-profile figures such as Keith Ellison to Congress, Somali Minnesotans realised they not only had the voting power to put their preferred candidate in high office; this candidate could even be one of their own. The first election experiment started at a local council in Minneapolis, when Abdi Warsame became the first Somali heritage councillor. This was followed by a number of state-level legislative elections where Somali-born Minnesotans secured seats, culminating in the election of Ilhan Omar – a Somali-born Minnesotan – to the US Congress. The views of Somali Minnesotans on US political and public life are shown below:

'We initially wanted to elect someone who will serve us well, then we thought to ourselves why elect others to higher offices when we can elect one of us.' (A Somali businessman)

132

'Seeing so many Somali-born Minnesotans win seats in higher places gives the young American-born Somalis the belief that America, despite its history, is inclusive.' (Member of state-level legislative)

'In America, with the right attitude and preparation, the sky is the limit. The best example is Ilhan Omar.' (High school student)

Not all that glitters is gold for Somali Minnesotans

Despite the success stories, Somalis in Minnesota face various challenges, as summarised below.

Succession problems

As the immigrant generation retires and loses control of critical social capital institutions, such as mosques and family businesses, the US-born generation is not yet ready or sufficiently disciplined to take over the community leadership:

'I fear if the trend continues the way it is [i.e. the generational gap] that we will end up with a less capable second generation of Somalis, and as a result the community would be at a loss.' (Somali father)

'We, the immigrant generations have done our bit to survive in American culture, but we may not have a replacement.' (Somali father)

Unemployment among Somali youth

Although Minnesota's unemployment rate remains relatively stable, unemployment among Somali youth is high, especially among boys. There are two reasons: most well-paid jobs require college degrees, and young Somalis, particularly those born in the US, are not willing to work hard in menial jobs.

Gang culture and substance misuse

Gang culture and substance misuse, resulting in prison sentences and even deaths, result not from external groups but occur among Somali gangs fighting over petty issues. Despite attempts by community leaders to resolve the problem, Somali boys are dying from gang violence as well opioid overdoses in shocking numbers.

Most victims of gang-related crimes are boys, but Somali girls are also involved: they are part of organised gangs but play a less conspicuous role than their male counterparts.

'Girls are part of the peer groups, they lead and help bait enemies, but they are not in the streets with us.' (Former gang member)

'My friend was killed by a trap set up by a Somali girl at a house party.' (Friend of a deceased Somali boy)

Although it is difficult to know why so many young Somalis boys are attracted to gang membership, a number of reasons are cited, as detailed below.

Fear

Young Somalis fear that if they are not members of a local gang, they may be vulnerable to street beatings or be suspected of being a member of a rival group:

'I was part of a gang who terrorised the streets, not because I wanted it, but out of fear of them, you either with them or against them.' (Former gang member)

Sense of belonging

Another key reason for Somali boys to join gangs is a sense of identity and a fear of being left out. Identity is very important in the formative years of boys, so they seek to be part of a group identity. As one former gang member explains:

'I was very much confused, ... had identity crises and wanted to be part of a group that represented me.' (Former gang member)

Failure breeds further failure

A common experience of Somali boys who become gang members is that they have all had negative experiences in school, from poor performance to exclusion:

> 'Most gang members have one thing in common, they all have had bad experiences at school.' (Somali boy)

> 'Gang membership is the only option open for you after you have been pushed out of school.' (Somali teacher)

Behind bars

Increasing numbers of Somalis boys are in state prisons serving sentences for crimes ranging from shoplifting to assault and armed robbery. In addition, substance use among Somali boys in Minnesota has been on the rise, resulting in multiple deaths. The combination of these two factors alone can create a lost generation.

Sending money to relatives

While remittances improve the well-being of family members left behind and boost the economies of the receiving countries, studies show that the dark side of remittance includes a culture of dependency in the receiving communities; it lowers labour participation rates and promotes conspicuous consumption.

Remittances are a universal experience in the Somali diaspora. Due to the informal channels used by Somalis to send money home, it is difficult to calculate exactly the total remittances sent, but the World Bank in 2016 estimated remittances to Somalia at USD 1.4 billion.

While remittances act as a crucial safety net for receivers in Somalia, they create a financial burden on the senders. The following quotes illustrate the financial drain caused by remittances among Somalis in Minnesota.

'My husband and I send every month at least USD500.00 to Somalia; some goes to his family and some goes to mine. This creates a lot of financial problems for us ... as we struggle to make ends meet.' (Mother of four)

'I am a single mum with 5 children to raise and I am still expected to send money to my relatives back in Somalia.' (Somali mother)

'If I invested all the money that I sent to Somalia in my own family here in Minneapolis, I would be financially secure for the rest of my life.' (Somali father)

'My father sends money every month to his family back home. While I understand the logic behind it, this money should have been put towards my college education.' (High school student)

'Why do you think so many Somali households rely on Section 8 and 9? The answer is remittance - it robs us of our chance of becoming homeowners.' (Somali father)

While remittance is generally seen as financial burden on families in the diaspora, some see it as their moral duty to help relatives left behind:

'We are very lucky to find ourselves in a rich country like America; we have food, we have shelter, but our relatives back home cannot say the same.' (Somali mother)

'Our remittance not only saves lives, but also serves a higher purpose, which is charity; we must help our needy relatives in Somalia.' (Somali father)

'There is a valid argument to have about the long-term effectiveness of monies we send back home, but the debate should not be whether we send or not.' (Somali teacher)

On Family and Parenting

Parenting style

Parenting, for most Somali parents, is predominantly focused on addressing the basic physiological needs of food, clothing and shelter. Parents also regard their responsibilities as including the education of their children, making sure they go to school on time and attend Quranic lessons or after-school classes at mosques. However, raising children involves more than meeting their physiological and educational needs. It involves emotional aspects, such as allowing the child to develop and grow as an individual. Many Somali parents either neglect this aspect, because they are physically or emotionally absent, or overdo it by overparenting, leaving their children without independent skills to stand on their own when the need comes.

Most fathers are either physically absent or psychologically detached from their sons' lives.

Somalis are by nature political, and the clan structures of Somali society allow division to flourish; most Somali fathers in Minnesota invest significant energy and time in the clan-based politics of Somalia, resulting in unsupervised homes and boys without male role models. Fathers may be physically absent or psychologically absent, that is, not emotionally present: their involvement in their boys' lives is limited to being physically present rather than actively shaping and taking part in the emotional lives of their sons.

Both absences are prevalent among Somali fathers. However, the first attracts more attention since the absence is physically felt at home. I asked a group of mothers about these two absences, and their anonymised responses are given below.

> 'My husband's absence is a physical one, he travels a lot; at times it feels that his priority lies in Somalia rather than his own family. The impact on the children is immense.' ('Kadija')

> 'My husband barely travels; he is always at home. However, he is psychologically absent, which means there is no meaningful engagement between him and his sons.' ('Halima')

> 'I would rather my children have a father at home rather than one that is absent, just being there physically makes lots of difference.' ('Rukia')

Fully involved father – revisiting Ilyas's story

The alternative to these two types of absence is to be fully involved in your sons' lives, both physically and psychologically. I will briefly recap the story of Ilyas, reported in Chapter 2:

> Ilyas is a father of four boys and one daughter. He is self-employed and, when not at work, he is at home with his children. He constantly communicates with his children's schools, ensures they complete

their schoolwork and keeps up-to-date through community centres with current issues affecting young people. He takes his children to sports and, by investing so much time in his children's education and social lives, he has become an important part of their daily lives. He feels the bond between him and his sons is stronger because they do so much together; they can ask each other anything and they discuss problems with school, friends or personal mistakes before they become an issue, so they can be nipped in the bud.

Ilyas is sympathetic to those who struggle to engage with their sons, especially those who are at home but psychologically not involved, because it is often the children, in their teens, who reject their fathers' attempts to be involved, seeking their own independence and identity. Ilyas believes that this puts many fathers off, and notes that fathers do not face the same problems with girls.

Ilyas's advice to fathers who are struggling to meaningfully involve themselves in their son's life:

'It is normal that your son in his teenage years is difficult to engage, they want their space, they want to be independent of you. This does not mean they hate you, or don't want to do anything with you — they do. Their worldview is different from yours,

bear with them, don't be judgmental, allow them to make managed mistakes, gentle persistence will eventually pay off.'

In addition to the invitation and resistance factor, the lack of 'economic freedom experienced by many Somali fathers impacts their involvement with their sons, as 'Mohamed' explains:

'Most of us work, sometimes two jobs. Because our jobs are not office-based, we do unsocial hours. When you do two shifts, you come home tired. It is also often the case that when working fathers come home, it is either a time when children are asleep or when they are at school. Economic freedom is what we lack, we can't choose our shifts and the time we work, this massively impacts on the time we spend with our children.'

Stages of growth

In his book *Raising Boys in the twenty-first century*, Steve Biddulph describes the three crucial stages of a boy growing up:

Birth to six when the boy 'primarily belongs to his mother'; the aim of this stage is to give the boy love and security and enable him to 'switch on' to life 'as a warm and welcoming experience'.

<u>Six to fourteen</u> when the boy starts wanting to learn to be a man. The father needs to build the 'competence, and skills' of his son, while helping him 'to become a balanced person' and to be happy and secure about being male.

<u>Fourteen to adult</u> where the boy wants to develop his own identity and to become his own man. He not only needs his father's support, but also 'input from male mentors if he is to complete the journey to being fully grown-up'.

According to my research, the most crucial stage for Somali boys is the second, although I would extend it to six to sixteen. It is now that Somali boys most need the involvement of their fathers, where they fall or succeed. Therefore, Somali fathers need to focus on the needs of their sons at this crucial stage. If they have psychologically and physically present fathers, boys develop confidence, model themselves on their fathers, and are likely to become 'happy and secure about being male'.

The second most crucial stage for Somali boys is the final stage, in the Somali case, from sixteen to adult. However, this stage barely exists for Somali boys in Minnesota; there are no known Somali heritage mentors to whom a father can take their sons. Having mentors at this stage will help Somali boys build cultural, spiritual and educational resilience, as Biddulph explains, 'joining more and more with the adult world'.

Most Somali fathers are emotionally and physically absent from their families. This absence damages their sons immensely, especially during the crucial stage between six and sixteen years.

Mothers do damage too

While Somali fathers who are absent or are less involved in their sons' lives damage the development of their sons, at the other end of the spectrum are mothers who over-parent their sons, with equally harmful outcomes. I identified two types of overparenting behaviour that Somali mothers engage in: helping without being asked and doing too much for their sons. See Chapter 2 for examples of each type.

Why are mothers overprotective of their sons?

I asked a group of Somali mothers in Minneapolis this provocative question, and these ideas emerged from their answers:

'Mothers have lots of fear about the well-being of their sons ... so they are naturally very protective of them.'

'America is very hostile for young black boys; they are vulnerable to the police, to the street and one another, hence mothers are very anxious.'

'Most fathers are absent, so what you see is psychologically mothers hanging on to their sons.'

'Most obsessions, fears and overprotective parenting behaviours by mothers to their sons also have something to do with their own childhood.'

These themes depict real issues on the ground. See Chapter 2 for more conceptualised examples.

Why do Somali mothers fear for their sons?

As discussed in Chapter 2, the US can be a hostile environment for black men, so Somali mothers have every reason to be anxious about the well-being of their sons, but this fear often prevents them from being rational. When mothers have irrational fears about the safety of their sons, they tend to over-parent and overprotect, which leaves the very children they wanted to protect unable to function independently in society. Parents told me about their moral panic related to their sons, fearing that they will become Americanised and even abandon Islam. Most of the Somali mothers I spoke to experience waves of moral panic and safety fears for their sons; these two factors are responsible for their overprotective parenting and, therefore, need to change.

Why Somali fathers need to watch boyhood stages

Biddulph's three stages of boyhood are useful in understanding the missing links in the parenting behaviours of Somali mothers and fathers. In the first stage from birth to six years old, mothers – who are primary caregivers – are overwhelmed with homemaking and household chores, leaving them too physically and mentally exhausted to fulfil their role of teaching their children about life and love. In the second stage, from the age of six, boys need the involvement of their fathers but, here too, Somali fathers are either absent or not involved in their sons' lives.

This failure by both parents to fulfil their respective roles has a negative effect on the early lives of Somali boys. In the teenage years, mothers suddenly recalibrate their roles, focusing on their sons with fear and anxiety. This sudden shift in parenting behaviour is triggered by two factors:

> *'Wiilasha markay yar yaryihiin ee ay guriga noo joogaan wax walwal ah nama hayo laakiin markay bilaabaan inay kaligood bixi karaan, cabsida markaas ayay nagu bilaabataa'* ['When our sons are young and at home, we don't worry. However, as soon as they start going out on their own, our fears kick in']. (Somali mother)

> *'Teenage boys often rebel, and the first person they rebel against are their mums; naturally,*

you want to keep them safe, so we [mothers] start overparenting and giving them everything they need to stop them rebelling more.' (Somali mother)

A solution to this problem is for parents to fulfil their appropriate roles earlier: if mothers have spent quality time with their sons from birth to 6 and fathers have been involved in their sons' lives thereafter, the problem would be reduced; boys would become robust and autonomous and develop relationships with their parents and others. Somali mothers need to be rational when dealing with their fears for their boys; fathers also need to watch the stages their sons go through from six to sixteen. The problems that manifest in the teenage years do not appear out of the blue; they have their origins as early as when the boys were six years old.

On Education and schooling.

Schools are one of the most important institutions in children's lives, second only to family. Most Somali children spend at least six hours each day in some form of school environment. In Chapter 2, I mentioned that Somali boys often have unpleasant experiences at school with both peers and teachers, and some of the key issues they face pivot around low expectations and the deficit model, racism and stereotypes. Below is a summary of the issues faced by Somali boys in the education system.

Schools' low expectations of Somali boys

Schools have low expectations of Somali boys, and believe that 'Somali ethnic groups do not value education and their children require more support in English.' A number of pupils explain below what they call 'schools' low expectations of Somali students':

'In my school, most of the students are white. The teachers automatically assume that the Somalians are not as clever as the other minority children, so they always treat me like illiterate.' (Somali boy)

'I'm not sure, but especially in math, the teachers automatically presume that I can't get anything higher than a B.' (Somali boy)

Linguistic and cultural deficit

The students' responses reveal teachers' and schools' negative attitudes towards Somali boys, but studies show that Somali girls face similar experiences. The deficit model emphasises what students lack in terms of cultural capital, but their cultural capital, such as bilingualism, is not valued. Below, Somali parents try to understand why schools attach less value to the cultural and linguistic capital of Somali pupils.

'I think the problem starts as early as pre-K, the average white kid comes with highly developed

vocabulary when they come to kindergarten, whereas Somali kids come with far too inferior English language skills; the label, therefore, has started years before kids start high school.' (Somali father)

'I would say there are elements of cultural racism from teachers against our sons. Schools see all immigrant students as low achievers.' (Somali mother)

'If students don't meet the socio-economic standards of white American teachers, the expectations automatically go down.' (Somali father)

Troublemakers

Almost all Somali boys feel schools treat them unfairly when it comes to classroom behaviour and general school discipline. They report that they are 'stereotyped by teachers as trouble-makers' and always find themselves in their 'teachers' books even if they had not done anything wrong'.

'Sometimes I feel like I'm getting labelled and I'm not sure why that is the case. I normally don't have any problems, but I get labelled as a troublemaker. If anything happens in the class - anything bad, I mean - I am the first student in the teachers' book. I think I feel I am going to hit an anger

*button the moment something like that happens.'
(Somali boy)*

I think Somalis stick up for one another and they react to situations quicker than others. Maybe the schools are racist or something; they never give us a chance. My friend, who is Somali and a very clever student, told me last year he was almost excluded because he was accused of calling a boy a 'white boy', and he said he is always called 'black', 'Muslim', and sometimes a 'pirate', and no one had done nothing about it.' (Somali boy)

'Sometimes you feel schools stereotype Somali kids and think that because our parents are from a war-torn country, so we are treated differently.' (Somali boy)

Racism

Racism in school is a common experience for most Somali boys. All the boys I met while researching this book had stories to tell about racism encountered in school settings. As of African descent, their skin colour plays an important role in the racism they encounter, but some boys think that their Somali culture and religion also make them target for racially motivated verbal abuse in schools.

'I am sick and tired of being told to go back where I came from? I was born in the US, yet I am told to go back to Somalia.' (Somali student)

'My friend and I are often called terrorists, pirates and religious fanatics.' (Somali student)

Low expectations, cultural and linguistic deficit, labelling as troublemakers, leading to expulsion and suspension

The problems of racism, low expectations and labelling Somali boys as troublemakers often lead to high suspension rates among Somali boys in the state's school system; students I spoke to fear being suspended from school by management, who often view Somali boys as 'badly behaved'. All those suspended or excluded from schools end up in some form of alternative provision, but parents view this as inadequate and feel let down.

'Once your son is suspended from school, he is done, forget about alternative schools, they offer no adequate teaching.' (Somali mother)

'My son was suspended from school and placed in a nearby alternative school, the teachers didn't bother about his attendance. They have never invited me to meet them and never sent me a school report – my son's education was forever damaged.' (Somali father)

'My son was suspended in dubious circumstances; they put him into alternative schooling, which offers

neither conducive learning nor a safe environment'
(Somali father)

Charter schools and Somalis

Although schools run by Somali management are mostly elementary and middle schools, the number of high schools is increasing. This means that more Somali students have access to these schools, attracted by two factors: 'language attachment' and 'culturally safe schooling'. Chapter 2 discusses these in more detail.

Key benefits of Charter schools

Language attachment

Parents new to the US, in particular, find communication with Somali-speaking school heads very helpful in their attempts to navigate the US school structure.

> *'Since I don't have enough knowledge about the education system of this country, I get help from the school leaders to answer all my educational questions about the school.' (Somali mother)*

> *'I speak English but it is not adequate enough to understand the educational needs of my children, hence Somali school leaders are my social capital.' (Somali father)*

'I don't have to complete a lengthy enrolment form on my own, I get this completed by the Somali-speaking professionals at school.' (Somali mother)

'Charter schools offer a great deal of support overall in the educational wellbeing of our children. I would recommend them to any parent.' (Somali father)

Culturally safe schooling

At the Charter schools, your kids are culturally safe while getting the same educational standards at any public school ... I am very happy for my children to be here. (Somali mother)

'My kids have no problem at school. No one calls them [racist] names and that is very reassuring.' (Somali mother)

'Even white teachers are culturally empowering; they want to know more about the Somali culture so that they can embed it in their lessons.' (Somali teaching assistant)

'Education that doesn't take the home culture into account is not an education in my view. Charter schools empower home culture.' (Somali father)

School-to-Prison Pipeline – revisiting the story of 'Farhan'

Farhan was a bright student in junior high, with a promising future. However, after race-related altercations with white students, his family transferred him to another high school, where the same problems recurred, but this time with teachers. He felt he was blamed for everything; the more he was in trouble, the angrier he became, and the more he reacted, the more he was in trouble.

After a verbal altercation with a teacher, Farhan was internally suspended but, according to Farhan's mother, the school failed to notify her of this. He was then given a final written warning but, again, according to his mother, this was not communicated to her. After a few months without incident, Farhan thought his troubles were behind him, but one lunchtime in the cafeteria, a racial insult escalated into a fight and the police were called. They arrested Farhan, the two white pupils who had started the fight and several others and, although they were all released on the following day without charge, one pupil pressed a charge that Farhan had 'broken his jaw', a claim Farhan, denies.

Farhan's mother was notified by the police that her son had been arrested and later learned of the charges pending. She was also told by the school board that he would be expelled and that a hearing date had been fixed. She did not know what to do but, on legal advice, decided not to appeal against the expulsion. Farhan was later found not guilty of the *charge, but was nevertheless expelled from his school. As is legally required, the state offered alternative education which his mother decided to accept.*

However, after a few weeks of attending the alternative school, Farhan started to skip classes and spend more time out with his friends. In her attempts to get Farhan off the streets and into school, his mother's relationship with him deteriorated and he did not always come home at night. He started to have an emotional and mental breakdown, and dropped out of the alternative school with no other options on the table. His promising future seemed to have vanished.

Farhan started smoking pot and experimenting with alcohol. He was arrested on several occasions but released without charge initially, until a raid on his home, after which he was charged with armed robbery and sentenced to ten years in prison. His story is not unique; it is one shared by many families, and illustrates the tragic experiences of Somali boys expelled from school without adequate alternative provision.

On how Somali boys are left behind

In Chapter 4, I mentioned that Somali girls perform better than Somali boys at school and in the labour market and asked why this should be the case?

My research identifies three factors that help Somali girls outperform Somali boys: parenting behaviours, the safety net and family honour, and schools' attitudes to black boys.

Parenting behaviours – early training

The different ways in which Somali girls and Somali boys are raised play a significant role in the life chances of the two genders. Girls are given early training by their mothers, while boys are left behind. At the age of six, gender characteristics start to appear: boys want to be boys and girls want to be girls. While mothers fulfil the needs of their daughters, boys tend to struggle, since fathers are generally either absent or not emotionally involved in their boys' lives.

> *'My daughter watches me every step of the way from a young age, she constantly learns from me, she benefits from my presence in the house.' (Somali mother)*

> *'I have two daughters and one son aged 7 years old. My husband is not at home all the time due to work, so while my daughters have their mum to learn from, my son has no one.' (Somali mother)*

> *'It is not that boys can't learn or be closer to their mothers, it is just their biological development that they want to do boys' stuff, hence the need for a male role model.' (Somali mother)*

'Most of us don't teach our boys what we teach our girls, such as cooking, cleaning, bed-making, because of the genderised nature of these chores.' (Somali mother)

Mothers do not deliberately or knowingly abandon their sons; they simply cannot fulfil the gender-related needs of boys from as early as six years old.

'Everything mothers teach their sons is gender-specific, a female perspective; this is fine for a period, but beyond that boys want to be a man, and here is where mothers' limitations start to appear.' (Kaaho)

'From the age of six, boys start to develop new interests: they want to play soccer, they want to play basketball, and they want to be boys. This is beyond our sphere of influence.' (Somali mother)

Family honour offers girls a safety net; boys have none

'The protection of family honour offers girls an extra safety net than boys.' (Somali father)

The safety net (see Chapter 4) is the product of a family code that demands Somali girls be 'culturally correct' and encourages them to stay away from anything that would tarnish the family's image in the community.

'My daughter is fully aware of the family honour on her shoulders, and she carries it well, but her friends see this as family control and are not too keen on the culture.' (Somali mother)

This expectation of carrying the family honour concentrates the minds of most Somali girls, making them take their responsibilities seriously:

'My daughter, thanks to her mother, dresses modestly, comes home early and is unlikely to hang out with friends aimlessly.' (Somali father)

Less grounded

Most Somali boys have no safety net for three specific reasons: first, they lack training from their mothers early in their lives and are deprived of empowering but straightforward skills such as cooking and cleaning. Second, most boys grow up in households where fathers are either physically or emotionally absent due to confused priorities; thus, they have no male role model to learn from. Third, in cultural terms, boys are not seen as a risk to the family image. Combine these reasons, and you find that boys in their teens have no safety net to protect them in life.

Difficulties at school

'Speak to any Somali boy in Minnesota, and they will tell you of an unpleasant school experience.' (Somali mother)

'While girls too suffer racism at school, boys have tough times; they are seen as out-of-control trouble-makers by teachers.' (Somali father)

Schools have the potential to make or break children. Unfortunately, Somali boys struggle in the school environment, particularly at secondary school. Schools see Somali boys in a negative light, which leads, at best, to poor performance or suspension and, at worst, exclusion.

To bring parity and help Somali boys catch up with Somali girls, I have suggested in Chapter 4 two key strategies: *fathers' early years involvement* and *mentorship programmes in teenage years.*

Early years – Why fathers matter

Boys need their fathers to be present physically and emotionally: they need to learn from them, they want to play with them, and most – from a young age – want to be like them. Numerous studies show that boys whose fathers are involved in their lives do better at school, attend college and become balanced adults. There is also new evidence to suggest that boys benefit psychologically from their fathers' involvement in their lives. For an illustration, see in Chapter 4 the story of the little boy who repeatedly became ill because of his father's extended absence.

Mentorship in teenage years

Mentorship of teenage boys is essential for their balanced and stable transition to adulthood. Unfortunately, Somalis lack this opportunity, one that I see as the missing bridge between teenage to adulthood for most Somali boys.

Why do I think mentorship is essential? This is why:

The ages between six and sixteen are crucial for your son. If you have been a meaningful part of your son's experience in these yours, you are likely now to have a balanced sixteen years old, confident in his male world. However, the most difficult times for any father start from the age of fourteen onwards when boys' hormones and physical growth mean they want to break into an adult world they are not yet ready to join. Even those fathers who were fully involved in their sons' lives find their sons become argumentative, develop selective hearing and are easily angered.

At this stage, fathers may see this as misbehaving and question their parenting techniques; they also become anxious about the risks brought by American pop culture, such as alcohol, drugs and crime. Instead of finding an outlet for their sons' energy, fathers tend to redouble their efforts to control through more schooling and more routine. Here, most relationships between teenage boys and their fathers break down. The best remedy is for fathers to stop emphasising the old routines – not allowing their sons to dictate but designing new activities to channel their creative energy and passion, and involving their sons in this process. In working with your son to design the next chapter, you need a third party to join you, and this is where mentors come in. Between the ages of 14 and 16, boys stop listening to their fathers, not because they hate them, but because they want to break away from the old routines of taking orders from their parents. Moreover, the relationship between fathers and their sons becomes tense and argumentative because two men are now involved. Bringing in a good and trustworthy mentor provides an extra balance.

See the story of 'Nat, Stan and the Motorbike' in Chapter 4.

Choosing a mentor for your son – what to look for

In Chapter 4, I offered some suggestions when choosing a mentor for your son, emphasising that the process must be led by the parents, and the person they choose to be a mentor for their son is a balanced adult who shares the wider interests their son may have, for example, a culturally and religiously competent person with an understanding of popular sports as well as popular culture.

I have mentioned a misconception among Somalis that mentors are like teachers, bridging the educational gaps of at-risk young people. This is not the case; a mentor is someone with certain experience and knowledge in a given domain who can motivate, train and advise their less-experienced mentee. A business owner can act as a mentor to a young person wanting a career in business, money management or investment; a retired teacher can mentor young boys aspiring to go to college or wanting a career in the education sector.

The benefits of a good mentor to your son

A good mentor can offer a number of benefits to your son, including constructive criticism, personal growth, a role model, encouragement and advice, trade skills, career guidance and networking connections. When choosing a mentor for your son, ensure that they are not acting as a supplementary tutor; they must have interests and expertise beyond formal education.

On culture and identity – the acculturation crisis

'I don't know my identity; I am conflicted. I am in-between I guess.' (Somali boy)

In Chapter 5, I explained that Somali boys' multi-hyphenated identities make it difficult for them to reconcile their home culture with the wider American culture. This causes conflicts within families; boys are wrongly accused of abandoning their culture when what is happening is an identity crisis. Boys are confused about their real identity or, to put it another way, which side of the hyphen they are on. This identity crisis is most acute during adolescence, and parents need to know that it is part of growing up in a culture and society that is different from the one they themselves grew up in, making their sons confused about their identity.

To understand the identity crisis Somali boys experience, and their attempts to negotiate these different cultures, see Chapter 5 for the story of 'Abdi' who uses a strategy he called 'jacket-switching'.

Parents' fear of acculturation

Somali parents have many fears and extreme emotions about their children's possible 'assimilation' into the wider American culture. They use a number of means to fight back, including individual cultural rehabilitation, popularly known as '*dhaqan celis*', or relocating the entire family to Somalia or a Muslim-majority country such as Egypt or Turkey. However, when these tools are used alone, they often fail to achieve the parents' desired goal of 'cultural correction'. To re-emphasise the failure of *dhaqan celis* and family relocation as a protection against assimilation, I want to re-visit the story of Nadiir (anonymised) who was sent to Kenya for cultural correction.

Nadiir's story

Nadiir was 14 when he started to argue with his parents, fight with his siblings and let his schoolwork slip. Despite his parents' moral panic, his teachers saw a good pupil with strong academic potential. However, he started skipping prayers, spoke less Somali at home and chose his own hairstyle. He was popular at school and had many friends of both genders and from all races. At home, he frequently stayed in his room playing on his Xbox console with friends online and offline. Nadiir's parents grew more and more anxious and, just before his 16th birthday, they decided to take him to Kenya on an extended vacation for cultural correction. To avoid Nadiir realising their plans, the whole family flew to Kenya on a family holiday, and Nadiir was very excited about visiting Africa for the first time and seeing his grandparents who lived there. After four weeks in Kenya, the rest of the family returned to Minnesota, but Nadiir and his father stayed on.

When Nadiir realised he was staying in Kenya indefinitely, he was angry and refused to speak to his parents for days. Eventually, he accepted his new home and was enrolled in a local school, where he seemed to have settled well. However, after his father returned to Minnesota, Nadiir started to miss school, hang out with other boys who had been sent back from Europe for cultural correction, and become involved with local gangs and the police. As time passed, Nadiir become too much for his grandparents, and his father had to return to Kenya.

Eventually, it was decided that Kenya was more dangerous to Nadiir than Minnesota, and Nadiir returned, after a year and a half, traumatised, angry with his parents and having missed two years of school.

Multi-hyphenated identity – The source of the problem

Their multi-hyphenated identity forces Somali boys to switch between cultures as they negotiate their position in society, for example, as Somali-Muslim-African-Americans. These identities compete with one another; some are approved by parents, others not. For example, parents encourage their sons to assume the Somali-Muslim elements, but are less keen on the African-American side. These competing identities and priorities are too heavy for Somali boys to carry. The problem is not the multi-hyphenated identity but, rather, the need to reconcile these elements or choose one over another while taking parents' wishes into account.

'Our parents don't understand that we are carrying identity weights on our shoulders; I have to be Somali, then Muslim, Black and then American. This is not an easy game.' (Somali boy)

'I don't want to disappoint my parents, but I also want to remain relevant in the dominant culture; how do you reconcile that?' (Somali boy)

'I truly want to be Somali, Muslim, Black and American, but I am only one person.' (Somali boy)

See Chapter 5 for more examples.

The cost of the identity crisis

One of the prices paid by Somali boys because of this identity crisis is mental illness, which is prevalent among Somali boys in Minnesota. While the causes vary, parents and community leaders believe that identity crisis is the biggest contributor. 'If a boy is confused and feels marginal to the dominant culture while not confident enough in his home culture, he may get angry or depressed, leading to other undesired habits such as doing drugs and drinking,' said one Somali teacher. To compound the problem, there is a stigma around mental illness among Somali Minnesotans and it is barely taken seriously until it is too late.

To illustrate this, I want to re-visit the story of 'Hussein', who was admitted to hospital and was still recovering from a serious mental illness at the time of writing, after experiencing what his parents described as a series of identity conflicts.

Hussein's story

Hussein was 17 at the time of the research. Just before his 16th birthday, he had started having problems at school, which led him to skip classes, and he was close to exclusion. His relationship with his parents and siblings had also begun to deteriorate: he constantly argued, refused to come straight home from school and often only returned very late at night. According to his parents, the problem was not only school; he had started listening to 'gangster music' at home, refused to pray and questioned his Islamic faith, his Somali culture and everything dear to his parents. They believed that he had started smoking. Just before his 17th birthday, Hussein began to behave more strangely and, one day, refused to leave his room, saying that someone was after him and would harm him.

His parents tried to take him to the doctor but Hussein refused their help; they tried to move him to Somalia to change environment but, again, he refused. As time passed, his health grew worse; he stopped taking a shower, brushing his teeth or eating, before starting to suffer hallucinations and panic attacks, and becoming suspicious of his own family. Finally, with the help of a family friend, Hussein was admitted to a psychiatric hospital, where he was diagnosed as suffering from serious mental health problems. At the time of writing, Hussein was recovering from his illness and taking antipsychotic medication at home.

Identity crisis – no joke

The identity crises facing Somali boys are real. All the Somali boys I surveyed were genuinely interested in maintaining their Somali culture, but were also interested in American culture and wanted to fit in with their peers. It is inevitable that, in trying to reconcile two opposing cultures, a crisis will emerge. Many Somali boys felt their parents lacked insight into their struggles, often dismissing identity crisis as a 'choice' that needs 'discipline'. A common response from parents is 'If the child is well disciplined, he should delineate boundaries between the two cultures', and make the 'correct choice'. For Somali boys, the correct choice often means 'rejection of the American side of the hyphen without a question'.

In Chapter 5, I suggested that, to remedy this, parents need to develop what I called 'contextual understanding': they need to understand that their sons live under a dominant culture, the American culture, which is globally pervasive and represents a very attractive and powerful brand in terms of entertainment, music and films. Somali boys find these aspects of the American culture appealing. I have also suggested that parents need to build a trust-based relationship with their sons in order to have frank conversations with them.

Somali boys in Minnesota – final thoughts

Between a rock and a hard place – family, schooling and identity

Somali boys face myriad challenges growing up in Minnesota – ranging from absent fathers and a lack of male role models to identity crises, hostile school systems and racism – and their experiences are shaped by these elements. In Chapter 2, I explained how absent fathers and overprotective mothers deprive Somali boys of strong foundations for facing life as young adults. Most importantly, from the ages of six to sixteen, the most important years, the lives of Somali boys lack direction.

In Chapter 3, I attempted to shed light on the schooling experiences of Somali boys, which do not make pleasant reading: hostile teachers, zero-tolerance school policies and widespread racism make school a miserable experience and, as a result of exclusion and suspension, many Somali boys do not receive an adequate education and find themselves in the juvenile criminal justice system.

Chapter 4 examines the contrasts between Somali boys and girls, and how factors such as the safety net, honour code, early training and school attitudes enable Somali girls to fare better than boys in education and work.

169

In Chapter 5, I addressed the struggles experienced by Somali boys when negotiating competing identities and the strategies they use to fit in with both family and peers.

From the outside, it is easy to become frustrated about how Minnesota-born Somali boys fall short of the expectations of their immigrant parents, who have succeeded despite the monumental challenges they faced. It is easy to call these at-risk young Somalis lazy and good for nothing. However, I argue that, having seen the problem at close quarters, what we see are the symptoms rather than the causes. Somali Minnesotan boys, and I refer here to those at-risk, are victims of what I call a deeply rooted triangle of death, in which family and school sit at the base of the triangle, with identity at the top (see diagram below).

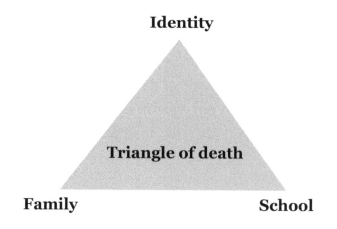

Identity

Triangle of death

Family   **School**

I offer below a further explanation of this triangle and how it contributes to the experiences of Somali boys.

Family Angle

Family is the most important institution for any child. Children need a stable and loving family if they are to lead balanced and fulfilling adult lives. While Somali parents work hard to meet the physiological needs of their children, they fail to meet their emotional needs, particularly of their boys. I argue that the ten years between the ages of six – when the boys want to be boys and decouple from their mothers, and sixteen when they want to be independent young men free from the shadow of their fathers are the most significant in the lives of Somali boys. The majority of Somali boys have to cope with parenting styles that fail to meet their needs in these ten years. Parents, and fathers in particular, are emotionally less invested in their sons, often either physically absent or emotionally disengaged, although emotional investment is more important than material investment for Somali boys.

What do I mean by emotional investment, and how this can be achieved by fathers? To invest emotionally in their sons' lives, fathers need first to be fully present, taking part in activities that support their child's emotional development, such as playing or watching sport, going on holidays, and hiking together. These activities are seen by children as rewards, rather than chores like schooling or other formal educational activities. This does not mean that the priority is playing rather than learning but, rather, that the child develops holistically, and becomes more balanced. It also cultivates closer emotional relationships between fathers and sons.

It is critical that emotional investment starts at the age of six and continues until the age of sixteen. At sixteen, as I explained, fathers must find reliable mentors for their sons to help them benefit from different perspectives. Mentorship plays an important role in boys' teenage years, when they are at the most confused stage of their lives, and eases potential tensions between fathers and their sons. At sixteen, boys want to be independent of their fathers, to design their own image, and there is nothing wrong with boys building their own individual identities if managed appropriately.

School

As discussed in Chapter 3, schools play an important role in the lives of Somali boys; after all, they spend six to seven hours each day in some form of school setting. While primary schooling presents few problems for boys, the story is different in secondary settings. Here, Somali boys face racism, suspension and exclusion, and stereotypes that label them as trouble-makers and academically weak. School–home communication is poor: when problems arise, parents are often not notified, or only after the damage has been done. Parents need to be aware that, for the majority of their sons, their educational needs are not met by schools and, in these cases, boys drift into street crime and gang membership. One way of resolving this is to liaise with the school your son attends, ask for feedback and school reports about his academic performance on a regular basis, and ensure you understand your rights as parents and your son's right to an education.

Identity

Somali boys navigate between multiple identities and face considerable peer, family and social pressure to conform in this regard. Parents demand that they remain Somali-Muslims, while their peers and society require them to be African-American. The result of this identity war is confusion at best and mental breakdown at worst. I have made some recommendations for dealing with boys when they are going through an identity crisis. However, the most important thing any parent can do is to spend time understanding the complexity of multi-hyphenated identity.

Selected Bibliography

1. Transnationalism among Second-Generation Muslim Americans: Being and Belonging in Their Transnational Social Field Michelle Byng, 2017

2. Trumped up Challenges: Limitations, opportunities, and the future of political research on Muslims Americans. Brian Robert Calfano, Nazita Lajevardi & Mellissa R. Michelson.

3. Outliers: The Story of Success. Malcolm Gladwell, 2009

4. Minnesota Employment and Economic Development: December 2019- Minnesota Employment Review online access: https://mn.gov/deed/newscenter/publications/ review/december-2019/

5. 'Monster in our Community': Easter African youth break the silence over addiction: Sahan Journal Online access: https://sahanjournal.com/changing-the-narrative/monster-in-our-community-east-african-youth-break-the-silence-over-addiction/

6. Maimbo, S.M (2006), Remittances and Economic Development in Somalia. Social development papers, conflict prevention and reconstruction paper No.38 Online Access https://www.cbd.int/financial/charity/

somalia-remittance.pdf & Lindley, A (2006); The influence of migration, remittances and diaspora donations on education in Somali society; Social development papers, conflict prevention and reconstruction paper No.38

7. Amuedo-Dorantes, C. The good and the bad in remittance flows. IZA World of Labor 2014: 97 doi: 10.15185/izawol.97 Online Access: https://wol.iza.org/uploads/articles/97/pdfs/good-and-bad-in-remittance-flows.pdf

8. Sir, hell is paved with good intentions- 1775 Samuel Johnson

9. National Low Income Housing Coalition: Public Housing History- Public housing timeline, 2019: https://nlihc.org/resource/public-housing-history

10. The Colour of Law A Forgotten History Of How Our Government Segregated America: Richard Rotchstein, 2018

11. More Housing Vouchers: Most Important Step to Help more People afford stable homes, 2021: Online access https://www.cbpp.org/research/housing/more-housing-vouchers-most-important-step-to-help-more-people-afford-stable-homes

12. Opportunity insights: Neighborhoods- Neighbordhoods Matter, 2014: Online Access: https://opportunity insights.org/neighborhoods/

13. Fatherhood Project: Why Fathers Matter. 2018. Online Access https://thefatheringproject.org/why-fathers-matter/

14. Life without Father. Popenoe, David, 1996. Online Access https://files.eric.ed.gov/fulltext/ED416035.pdf

15. Raising Boys in the 21st Century: Completely updated and revised: Steve Biddulph, 2018.

16. Breathe: A letter to My Sons. Imani Perry, 2019

17. How to Raise Successful People: Simple lessons for radical results. Esther Wojcicki. 2019.

18. The School- to- Prison Pipeline: Structuring Legal Reforms: Catherine Y. Kim, Daniel J Losen, and Damon T. Hewitt.

19. Defining Genealogies: Feminist Reflections on being South Asian in North America," in *Our Feet Walk the Sky, Writings by Women of the South Asian Diaspora,* CA: Aunt Lute Books, 1993.

20. Hyphenated Identities: The Challenges of Living in-between. Raluca Popescu. 2012

21. Islam in the United Sates of America. Sulayman S. Nyang. 1990

Milton Keynes UK
Ingram Content Group UK Ltd.
UKHW011512160624
444162UK00001B/31